R.A. Keeling.

Imagined land

ESSEX IN POETRY
AND PROSE

Imagined land

ESSEX IN POETRY
AND PROSE

by Bill and Sue Liddell

Photographs by Keith Mirams

Essex Record Office
Chelmsford, 1996

Published by the
ESSEX RECORD OFFICE
County Hall, Chelmsford, Essex CM1 1LX

© Essex County Council, 1996

All rights reserved – This book may not be reproduced,
in whole or in part, in any form,
without permission from the publishers

British Library Cataloguing in Publication Data
A catalogue record for this book is available from the British Library

ISBN 1 898529 10 8

Essex Record Office Publication No. 135

Mirams Design
Printed by The Lavenham Press Limited

Contents

Preface page vii

A sense of place page 1

The landscape of Essex page 7

Marshland and estuary page 17

The forest page 27

Champion country page 35

Townscapes page 41

People and work page 61

Acknowledgements page 78

Index of authors page 79

List of illustrations

Front cover:	River Stour at Dedham
Back cover:	Ramsey's Mill at Dovercourt
Frontispiece	Estuary mud at Maldon
facing p. viii	River crossing to the wider world: Queen Elizabeth II Bridge
facing p. 1	Woodland's edge
p. 5	Pastoral idyll: echoes of prosperity based on wool
p. 6	Arable land in the Tendring Hundred
p. 15	Eroded foreshore on the Blackwater estuary
p. 16	Derelict oyster smack at Tollesbury
p. 19	Estuary evening
p. 22	The power of the North Sea
p. 26	Ancient woodland at High Beech, Epping Forest
p. 33	Monks Lane between Ardleigh and Dedham
p. 34	Secluded valley
p. 40	The Dutch Quarter, Colchester
p. 43	Snow scene from the Castle ramparts, Colchester
p. 47	Harwich harbour
p. 49	Southend highlights
p. 52	Fun in the surf at Walton-on-the-Naze
p. 55	Waltham Abbey
p. 61	Essex sailing barges
p. 65	Bait-digging at West Mersea
p. 69	Sail lofts at Tollesbury
p. 70	Blacksmith
p. 73	Courthauld's Town Mill, Halstead
p. 77	John Webb's mill at Thaxted

Preface

IN 1988 THE Essex History Fair at Tilbury Fort had, as part of its programme, a series of lectures about aspects of Essex: and one of the lectures was on Essex writers. This lecture had been prompted by a reading of an article by the travel writer, Norman Lewis, who had lived in and written about Essex. He commented on the unattractive aspects of the landscape and on the foreign, alien, hidden elements of the people. These comments provoked our research into what other writers had to say about the county; this book grew out of that research, set against a background knowledge of the local and regional history of Essex.

It is a book about Essex as it has developed – the settlements, the countryside, the seascape, the people – an attempt to show the links between what we see and what we read; between the landscape as people have made and fashioned it over the centuries and the literature that has tried to describe the effect these changes have had on places and people. It depicts the county of Essex as it has been observed and written about over the years.

It is a book about Essex and the imagination – scenes, descriptions, thoughts – aimed at linking reader and writer in responding to the world about them; in 'reading' the landscape. One of the background works consulted, *The Poetry of Habitat* by Jay Appleton, includes the comment 'Landscape is a kind of backcloth to the whole stage of human activity', and the book does centre on human life, set against literary descriptions that evoke the pleasure, the danger, the excitement or the everyday elements of the landscape.

It is a book of quotations about Essex both visual and literary – from diaries, poems, novels, travel accounts and so on – an introduction, or re-introduction, to the county by authors and artists who may not all be writers of literature in the strict sense of the word, but who are all part of that company that find Essex a place that inspires affection and irritation, fondness and exasperation, admiration and criticism; a place that Norman Lewis can still, after years of living and working elsewhere, refer to as 'home'.

It is a book that has given us an enormous amount of pleasure to work on – researching, finding out, looking up, chasing after. It has introduced us to or reminded us of many writers, all of whom we have enjoyed reading, but not all of whom have we been able to include. It has provided us with an excuse to sit and read, and a reason to go out and observe; it has made us look at the maps of Essex in a new way and think about the landscape in a different light.

And it has involved us with a variety of people for whose help and assistance we are grateful and to whom we would like to give our thanks – Vic Gray, Janet Smith, the staff of the Essex Record Office, Keith Mirams the book's designer and photographer, Ernest Fulcher, Ann Padfield and members of various groups and societies around the county in Billericay, Epping, Halstead, Wansfell College and Debden House. We wish to give special thanks to the Friends of Historic Essex for their generous help with production costs.

A sense of place

LIKE GREAT BRITAIN, like England, Essex has a mystique that remains private and invisible, but which can be glimpsed in a variety of individual characteristic regions.

To some extent it is divided because of its geological patterns and land usage, and the divisions are reflected in literature in three main well-established areas: the marshland and estuary; the forest; the champion country of central and north-west Essex; and a fourth: urban and built-up Essex. These are worlds where invasion, mystery and adventure lurk by the sea; where safety, escape and danger mingle between the trees; where hard work and fertile soil produce crops and prosperity; and where commuting and development create a desire for countryside and peace.

Essex is a composite county, whose regions have been viewed and written about as if each of them were the whole, or as if they made a miscellany, not a whole. So to H G Wells it was "a characteristic and individualised county which wins the heart"; to William Addison it was "a county of contrasts"; yet Norman Lewis could simplify its complexity and say "Essex is the ugliest county". There is some truth in each of these definitions, but we still ask how can such a county be typified? It is the second largest administrative county in the country; it is the envy of many and it is the butt of innumerable jokes; it is the land of thousands of commuters and the hidden home of thousands who stay and work locally; it is an unseen and unknown territory to those who cross its surface by train, car or lorry. Can such a county have a unified existence?

> "The County of Essex is one of the best situated in this kingdom, on account of its nearness to the capital, convenience of water-carriage, good roads in general and other great advantages. This county is not filled with light stands, apt to be blown about with every high wind; nor is it covered with barren rocks, or dreary mountains; but the surface of it is, in general, level. However, it is not dead flat, but diversified with agreeable eminences and fruitful dales ... The country being enclosed, makes it much more comfortable to live and travel in."
>
> *Philip Morant* The History of Essex, *1768*

Attempts to define 'Essex' and 'Essexness' reveal a central difficulty, for the unified Essex exists only in the imagination. Who has seen the whole landscape, except from the air? For each individual, the county is composed of 'hidden' realities based in imagination, tradition and legend. Here there is a world whose landscape is compound of hills, woods, fields edged by trees, marshlands, estuaries and rivers, appearing and disappearing, all invisibly moving into the sea, from which rises the overarching sky – the ever-present Essex sky that transmutes this variety into a kaleidoscopic unity represented (wrongly) by so many as a flat and boring land; yet to those who know it, a land of views and vistas.

As one travels around, the county's imaginative unity breaks up into diversely individual and particular views, which are preserved in literary form and discourse in a mixture of descriptive styles and languages. All of these differ through time, yet all encircle a central secret quality that is mytho-poetic and magical – a mystery:

> "Perhaps, of all the counties of England, the one which is least known by English people generally is the county of Essex."
>
> *Frances C Burmester* John Lott's Alice, *1902*

In this landscape of the imagination there are many stories. Starting in Roman times with the tale of brave Boudicca and her daughters spurning the humiliation of 'slavery' in favour of heroic failure in battle against the Romans, the legend of the fiercely independent and separate people of Essex grew. The story of Boudicca has been eagerly seized upon by Essex writers like George Walker in his *The History of a Little Town* (Billericay) to exaggerate the importance of place:

> "The final defeat of Boadicea was between Colchester and London, again we can only guess how near to Billericay was the final battle. Whether the final defeat was just outside the Roman fort at Norsey Wood, or much nearer Colchester, some of the fighting between Roman and Celt was near Billericay and the statue of Boadicea in her war chariot on Westminster Bridge is another of the memorials of the past in which the old town has special interest."
>
> *George Walker* The History of a Little Town, *1947*

This union of independence and defeat echoes through the centuries, revealing the strong local ties that bind the people of Essex to their 'place'. The English messenger in 'The Battle of Maldon' poem states it defiantly:

> "Pirates' messenger, deliver and say to your people the more hateful tale that here stands a famous earl with his forces, who will defend *this land*, the country of Ethelred, *the people and the ground.*"
>
> *8th century, authors' translation and emphasis*

In exile in the twentieth century the Essex-born American writer, Denise Levertov, reflected on such local ties to origin and birth-place:

A SENSE OF PLACE

"who now in a far country
remembers the first river, the first
field, bricks, and lumber dumped in it ready for building,
that new smell, and remembers
the wall of the garden, the first light."
Denise Levertov A Map of the Western Part of the County of Essex in England, *1958*

That this county was and is a garden was noted early. One of its principal functions as a geographical area has always been to provide for London, its one-time metropolis as Bede tells us, and this was a well-established part of the county's life by the sixteenth century:

"This shire is moste fatt, frutefull, and full of profitable things,
exceding (as farr as I can finde) anie other shire, for the generall
comodeties ... this shire seemeth to me to deserve the title of the englishe
Goshen, (place of light and plenty) the fattest of the Lande: comparable
to Palestina, that flowed with milke and hunnye."
John Norden Description of Essex, *1594*

This agricultural past (and present) has so shaped the landscape that the divisions of this book reflect it: the marshlands, the wood pasture and the champion region of mixed husbandry as the economic historians define it. This scene was created over thousands of years, shaped by the people who occupied it and formed a landscape of independent parishes that many glory in and wonder at today:

"It is, moreover, a remarkable county from the number of districts it comprises, all closely abutting on one another, and yet each so absolutely distinct and separate from the others, that I, who until a few years ago lived my whole life in one part, should find myself an utter stranger elsewhere, hardly understanding the tongue that was spoken to me."
Frances C Burmester John Lott's Alice, *1902*

This county has also produced and still produces a variety of literature. Some of its writers, born and bred in Essex, feel it as an inspiration of their art; others, from outside the county, feel a need to describe the territory and its past to the world at large. It is as if Essex, the kingdom of the East Saxons – not Anglian, not London – calls on them to explain its differences. Yet, wherever they come from, all these writers present Essex stories, Essex themes, Essex characters and the Essex countryside in terms of the particular – particular settlements of particular areas in different epochs. In other counties particular writers comment on their own times, or the immediate past, and create a county image, a symbolic scene, which then becomes the accepted, if imagined, truth about the area – Wordsworth's Lakeland, the Bronte's Yorkshire, or Thomas Hardy's Wessex. In Essex, writers have produced works that show a concern to depict the variety and diversity of the world around them, whether it be their contemporary world or an imagined world of the past, in woodland or as vista:

> "King Sighere ... and his troop of men-at-arms were riding, their bare heads unhelmeted, their battle-axes laid carelessly across their saddles, never dreaming of danger in this, their own East Saxon land ... The forest here was thinning to its outskirts and through the trees could be caught glimpses of a wide country ... It was a fair scene of peace and plenty."
>
> *Kate Thompson Sizer* The Wooing of Osyth: the Story of the Eastern Counties in Saxon Times, *1934*

There is no one Essex, for no one writer has been able to impose a singular view upon it. No town or district, except possibly London, dominates its variety. Its diversity and absence of uniformity is its especial charm. In its myriad particularities, Essex is exalted; we hope that in this book we have reflected something of that entrancing intricacy and complexity.

The landscape of Essex

THE LANDSCAPE OF Essex may be a multifarious one, but what is meant by the word landscape? By and large the word refers to the countryside – the pastoral, rural, rustic, country scene – and by and large this is what the literature of Essex shows us. Pictures of trees and woods, fields and flowers, rivers, streams and seashores abound in English literature, for the pastoral tradition is very English. It is a tradition that links a person's own experience and use of the countryside with the way everyone records and arranges sensations and feelings about nature and the natural world.

This natural world which we view began thousands of years ago, as William Addison explains:

"The Essex landscape is uniquely the creation of glacial drifts that reached the north-east of the county at the end of the Ice Age, and in gliding southwards either split to form inland lakes, or pressed forward to gouge out channels for slow meandering rivers."
William Addison 'The Making of the Essex Landscape' *from* An Essex Tribute, *1987*

Like all writers, Essex writers have used the landscape of water to provide a background, to create a mood, to comment on mankind's ways, to establish continuity, to present a refuge or to show men and women at work.

The romantic idyllic Arcadia of Essex is often linked with its rivers and streams, and no one shows this link more clearly than Michael Drayton in 'Polyolbion' as he leads the reader through the Essex waterways:

"Fools gaze at painted courts, to th' country let me go,
To climb the easy hill, then walk the valley low;
No gold-embossed roofs to me are like the woods;
No bed is like the grass, no liquor like the floods ...
For Essex is our dower, this greatly doth abound
With every simple good, that in the Ile is found ...
When Hatfield taking heart, where late she sadly stood,
Sends little Roding forth, her best-beloved Flood;
Which from her crystal fount, as to enlarge her fame,
To many a village lends her dear and noble name ...
From whose vast beechy banks a rumour straight resounds,

IMAGINED LAND

> Which quickly ran itself through the Essexian grounds,
> That Crouch amongst the rest, a River's name should seek,
> As scorning any more the nickname of a Creek,
> Well furnished with a stream, that from the fill to fall,
> Wants nothing that a flood should be adorned withall.
> Choice Chelmer comes along, a Nymph most neatly clear,
> Which well-near through the midst doth cut the wealthy sheere ...
> Clear Can communes tripping in, and doth the Chelmer close ...
> When Chelmer scarce arrives in her most wish'd bay,
> But Blackwater comes in, through many a crooked way,
> Which Pant was called of yore; but that, by Time exiled,
> She Freshwell after hight, then Blackwater instyled.
> But Colne, which frankly lends fair Colchester her name ...
> At mighty Neptune's beck, thus ended they their song,
> When as from Harwich all to Loving-land along,
> Great claps and shouts were heard resounding to the shore,
> Wherewith th'Essexian nymphs applaud their loved Stour."
>
> *Michael Drayton* 'Polyolbion', *1622*

But central to the life and work of Essex in the past, and to the vistas of Essex in the present, are the trees, in particular the elms – a distinctive feature of the Essex landscape – distinctive for their idiosyncratic growth and durability:

> "for they grow ... in crooked maner, that they are almost apt for nothing else but navie timber, great ordinance and beetels; and such thereto is their naturall qualitie, that being used in the said behalfe, they continue longer and more lone than anie the like trees in whatsoever parcell else of this land, without cuphar, shaking or cleaving, as I find."
>
> *William Harrison* Description of England, *1587*

distinctive also for their provision of space for romantic meetings:

> "In the parish there stood at the date of my lay
> Three mighty elm pollards, and do to this day -
> Gnarled, knotted, and knaggy, as anyone may
> Observe at this moment – a view 'twill repay;
> They're enormous in bulk, hollowed out by decay ...
>   And here when the Moon
>   Shone brightly in June
> 'Twas a glorious place for two lovers to spoon,
> - Or list to the nightingale trilling a tune."
>
> *JFTW* 'A Legend of Paglesham', *1888*

as well as for their links with the history of the county:

"The stately church of Finchingfield, associated with memories of Stephen Marshall, the famous Puritan preacher in the days of the Commonwealth, is sheltered by some magnificent elms, which may have witnessed the changes of that stirring time. In that same neighbourhood, the peaceful churchyard of Black Notley is separated from the adjoining cornfields by a long line of ancient elms, which stand sentry over the pyramidal tomb, erected to the memory of our illustrious naturalist, John Ray."
John Vaughan Lighter Studies of a Country Rector, *1909*

and their stubborn individuality when it comes to reproduction:

"I often wonders about they owd Elums
'Ow they seems ter git everywhers
T'aint as if 'em seeds, like other trees
'Em just runs they owd roots un'erground
Ar-a do-an-all, fifty t'sixty foot odd,
Then up they shoots a little clump 'er Elum suckers,
Make a little spinny on 'em a do in time
Then off 'em goes agin, when trunks is big 'nough
For another fifty t'sixty foot, an'a nother spinny …
But say what yer like, they be queer, owd trees."
A G Harknett 'Elms' *from* Thoughts for Pleasure, *20th century*

Like the county itself, the elms show a tenacity, sturdiness and zest for life, despite physical setbacks, that have been present in the landscape for centuries. So John Norden describing the county in 1594 neatly sets the good alongside the bad, and comes up with the conclusion that the good outweighs the bad; the fertile fields and pastures overcoming the fever:

"But I can not comende the healthfullness of it: And especiallie nere the sea coastes, Rochford, Denge, Tendering hundredes and other lowe places about the creekes, which gave me a moste cruell quarterne fever. But the manie and sweete comodeties countervayle the daunger."
John Norden Description of Essex, *1594*

This seems to be the case with Essex writers since then for there is an acceptance of the reality of life in the Essex landscape. J G O'Leary wrote "Essex must be viewed as a whole, warts and all", echoing again the classical pastoral tradition that sees the dual role of the countryside – the soft and the hard:

"The 'soft' pastoral is a romance, a dream of celebration, carnival, song and love ... it can be elegiac as well as idyllic ... The other kind of pastoral admits that the rural life is 'hard'; it is a realist narrative of labour and endurance."
Hermione Lee Willa Cather: A Life Saved Up, *1992*

The celebration of the landscape and beauties of the countryside declined somewhat during the eighteenth century when rural life was seen as dull and boring in comparison with the sophistication and civilisation of the town, and the country people were "so abject and sordid in temper they seem almost to have undergone poor Nebuchadnezzar's fate and by conversing continually with the beasts to have learned their manners" (quoted by Keith Thomas in *Man and the Natural World*, 1983). This was a time when nature and the landscape were to be moulded and fashioned by men:

"It is a common observation that the wise and bountiful Author of nature has so blended his works together, that even those we are apt to find fault with have their peculiar advantages; thus the marshy grounds in Essex afford excellent pasture; nor is there a county in England where provisions in general are in greater plenty. The London markets are supplied by Essex with vast quantities of corn, and great numbers of oxen, calves and sheep; they also breed great numbers of horses, and the fish, particularly oysters, bring vast sums annually to the county; there are great numbers of wildfowl near the Thames which are sold in London to the dealers."
The New British Traveller, *1724-1794*

So by the nineteenth century, the agricultural prosperity of Essex was well established and the landscape , though more diversified, was still rural:

"Agriculture, which has much improved the face of the county, is the principal feature of it, the produce of which consists of livestock, chiefly calves (for their goodness Essex has long been proverbial) besides the finest wheat flour and all other kinds of grains and hops, coriander, caraway, saffron, teazle, etc."
P Youngman Excursions in the County of Essex, *1818*

and especially in the north, now that the woollen industry had died, it was acquiring the romance and mystery of hidden elusive seclusion:

"I hardly know any county with the rural and secluded character of north Essex. It seems immensely old, and is full of old halls and woods and hollows and low ranges of hills, and then eight or nine miles off, across the deeply quiet part of the county is the sea."
Matthew Arnold on a visit to Copford in 1861

THE LANDSCAPE OF ESSEX

By the nineteenth century there was also emerging an appreciation of the seashore landscape of Essex – not the damp aguish world of the marshes, but the world of sea and ships, sailors and adventurers, where Essex provided a refuge from the increasing rigours of industrialised society and work:

"In Essex there is greater tranquillity, if less conspicuous beauty. The waterways are more diversified, go farther into the land and offer more unusual aspects than the Medway, the only really navigable river on the north shore. Essex is, comparatively, an unknown land. Its quiet beauties and splendid views have not often been sung ... Few counties have finer manor houses, more magnificent monumental tombs, timber work of a nobler architectural character, than Essex. The country is hilly in many parts. The views from the Laindon Hills, Hadleigh Castle, Danbury Church, Ashingdon and Great Totham have a beauty and extent all their own."

Frank Cowper Sailing Tours, *1892*

By the twentieth century, therefore, Essex and its rural landscape was seen by many, especially Londoners, as an ideal; the classical view of the countryside as the lost Garden of Eden; the idealised image of the Golden Age; the nostalgic home of innocence and childhood. And this ideal was increasingly reflected in literature.

Edward Thomas, for example, who brought his family to live in Essex during the First World War, became enchanted by the names of the places and the seemingly untroubled eternities of the countryside – woods, fields, ponds, birds – and created a poem that lilts to a nursery rhyme rhythm:

"If I were to own this countryside
As far as a man in a day could ride,
And the Tyes were mine for giving or letting, -
Wingle Tye and Margaretting
Tye, – and Skreens, Gooshays, and Cockerells,
Shellow, Rochetts, Bandish and Pickerells,
Martins, Lambkins, and Lillyputs,
Their copses, ponds, roads and ruts,
Fields where plough horses steam and plovers
Fling and whimper, hedges that lovers
Love, and orchards, shrubberies, walls
Where the sun untroubled by north wind falls,
And single trees where the thrush sings well
His proverbs untranslatable,
I would give them all to my son
If he would let me any one

For a song, a blackbird's song, at dawn."
Edward Thomas 'To Merfyn', *1916*

H G Wells saw beyond childhood to the historical and magnificent landscape of the past in Essex where danger and hazard lurked beyond the security of moat and armour; he compared the south of the river with Essex:

"Essex is so much more genuinely Old England than Surrey, say, or Kent. Round here you'll find Corners, and Fairlies and then you get Capels, and then away down towards Dunmow and Braintree Maynards and Byngs. And there are oaks and hornbeams in the park about Clavering that have echoed to the howling of wolves and the clank of men in armour. All the old farms here are moated – because of the wolves. Clavering itself is Tudor, and rather fine too. And the cottages still wear thatch."
H G Wells Mr Britling Sees it Through, *1916*

and roses round the door! A lost garden of Eden indeed; a world that is now a by-gone age, as John Betjeman saw it in its Edwardian splendour:

"The deepest Essex few explore
   Where steepest thatch is sunk in flowers
And out of elm and sycamore
   Rise flinty fifteenth century towers.

I see the little branch line go
   By white farms roofed in red and brown,
The old Great Eastern winding slow
   To some forgotten country town.

Now yarrow chokes the railway track,
   Brambles obliterate the stile,
No motor coach can take me back
   To that Edwardian 'erstwhile'."

John Betjeman 'Essex', *1954*

Against this elegiac and melancholic view of the passing of an idyllic landscape can be set the 'alternative' landscape of Essex, the harsh realities of endurance in a hostile environment. John Norden in the sixteenth century had pointed out the unhealthy atmosphere, an aspect of the county picked out by Daniel Defoe and the *New British Traveller* in the eighteenth century and embellished in the nineteenth by Charles Dickens in *Great Expectations* to give a picture of an unattractive, stagnant and depressing landscape:

THE LANDSCAPE OF ESSEX

"It was like my own marsh country, flat and monotonous ... Some ballast-lighters, shaped like a child's first rude imitation of a boat, lay low in the mud; and a little squat shoal-lighthouse, on open piles, stood crippled in the mud on stilts and crutches; and slimy stakes stuck out of the mud, and red landmarks and tidemarks stuck out of the mud, and an old landing-stage and an old roofless building slipped into the mud, and all about us was stagnation and mud."

Charles Dickens Great Expectations, *1860-61*

This feature of the marshland landscape – depressing, monotonous but with slightly sinister overtones – is picked up again in the twentieth century by such writers as Margery Allingham and June Thompson; and the occasionally unattractive aspects are given an environmental slant by Norman Lewis:

"In true Essex style there had been no attempt to tidy up before departure, and so now a half dismantled pump protruded from the water and rails carried several shattered trucks down to the bullrushes sprouting on the verge of what was now a small lake; there were old breeze-blocks, oil barrels, a wheel-less vehicle sitting on its springs, and iron gates that opened wide upon further devastation. All these objects were host to the rank but vigorous creeping plants that would eventually muffle their outlines with coarse leaves and insignificant flowers."

Norman Lewis 'Essex' *from* Granta *Vol. 23, 1988*

and a bureaucratic, regimented emphasis by Angus Wilson:

"But even if there were some stray clumps of wild flowers in Gorman's Wood, Sylvia could not find them, for the only footpath was cut off from the trees on each side by close-meshed fence ... She walked on past neat ovals in which newly bedded plants as yet not in flower were protected in their soggy hollows by a surround of wire hoops ... After four or five days of such frustrated assaults upon the countryside, she came one afternoon upon a signpost that read merely "Footpath" and, after a sceptical quarter of an hour, she realised that she was at last moving away from the town along a path that was no more than a narrow grass strip between two sown fields."

Angus Wilson Late Call, *1964*

As O'Leary said, the Essex landscape has to be taken 'warts and all', especially in the twentieth century; but all is not lost. In a County publication in 1978 a teenager wrote a hopeful and comprehensive landscape of the county:

IMAGINED LAND

"Essex is a nice old county,
Rivers and streams racing through,
The Thames, Crouch, Chelmer and Blackwater
bite into Essex from the sea.
Dotted about Essex are stately homes and museums.
The beaches of Southend are great fun.
So are the theatres, swimming pools and
sports centres as well.
I like Essex."

Stephen Farrar We Live in Essex *1978*

Marshland and estuary

A TRAVELLER, MOVING from west to east across southern England, may well be aware of an air of expectancy, a sense of alertness, a feeling of being on the 'qui vive', of being prepared for anything, that permeates the eastern counties, and in none more so than the county of Essex. The same traveller, looking at the county from across the Channel, would notice the enticing inlets and estuaries that tempt and beckon invasion. And Essex has been invaded several times:

"There is a land that has a Saxon heart,
Where language of the Latinate is least,
Where Nordic with a tongue of salt is cast
On level lines towards the Northern seas."
Mervyn Linford 'Glaucous Gold', *1984*

It is a county that has survived the onslaught of Roman, Saxon, Viking and Norman conquest. So it is not surprising that an air of expectation and anticipation prevails, for the county has had to face not only these human invasions, but also invasion by the sea:

"Essex and the sea have been antagonists for centuries. 'On the east' wrote John Norden, the Elizabethan topographer, Essex 'encountreth the mayne Ocean, an infallable bounde.' Ceaselessly the conflict born of that encounter flows backwards and forwards with the tide. The creeks, estuaries and rivers of the Essex coast – Stour and Colne, Blackwater, Crouch and Roach, Thames, Ingrebourne, Roding and Lea – are arms of the sea restlessly probing the heart of the county. To William Camden, another Elizabethan topographer, it seemed that 'the Ocean windeth itself into it'. The geographical area of the county is 1,528 square miles, but no point lies more than thirty-four miles from tidal water."
Hilda Grieve The Great Tide, *1959*

This proximity to the sea produces a combination of active, prosaic descriptions and thoughtful, slightly melancholy reflections about the area, as in this extract from Hervey Benham where past, present and future are linked by the tides:

"And through all its creeks and inlets the tides ebb and flow as they have since time began – through all the 'bays, channels, roads, bars, strands, harbours, rivers, streams, creeks and places within the said limits contained', as the old Customs records put it. They are the very pulse-beat of eternity, the tides, and to dwell awhile in a realm ruled by their unchanging, unhasting tempo guides the mind, uneasily attuned to the fevered rhythm of a modern world, into a contemplation of things wide and infinite, a sympathy with natural forces which is an experience as profound, stimulating and satisfying as a man can know."

Hervey Benham The Last Stronghold of Sail, *1948*

and its poetic equivalent by Mervyn Linford:

"This ooze that in the miracle of light
Can seem as though eternity in time
Will sudden turn to dark on lowering sky
And leave the soul so desolate and blind,
And yet, these bleak horizons hold me still,
No risen scarp can move my leaden faith,
No undulated wealth of upland fields
Could buy the rich seclusion of this place,
This glaucous gold is all that I could wish,
The spirit's voice on skeins of endless geese.
Alluvial, the thought that through the mist
Attaches shape to solitary trees."

Mervyn Linford 'Glaucous Gold', *1984*

Reflecting in tide and time on the Essex coastline prompts writers to comment on the appearance of stretches of water as backdrop or backcloth to narrative events. Sabine Baring-Gould (1834-1924) opens his novel *Mehalah* with a picture of the marsh:

"Between the mouths of the Blackwater and the Colne, on the east coast of Essex, lies an extensive marshy tract veined and freckled in every part with water. At high tides the appearance is that of a vast surface of Sargasso weed floating on the sea, with rents and patches of shining water traversing and dappling it in all directions. The creeks, some of considerable length and breadth, extend many miles inland, and are arteries whence branches out a fibrous tissue of smaller channels, flushed with water twice in twenty-four hours. At noontides, and especially at the equinoxes, the sea asserts its royalty over this vast region."

Sabine Baring-Gould Mehalah: A Story of the Salt Marshes, *1880*

The reference to the Sargasso Sea gives a universal depth to the scene, whilst the precise details of the tide times enhances the local flavour – both elements central to the unfolding of the story.

On a much more humorous note the writer with the pen name JFTW comments on that other significant feature of the Essex coastline – the mud:

"Square
And massive this castle of Hadleigh stood – There
Now are its ruins, at which you may stare
As you travel by railway, or down the Thames scud
From London to Southend on – shall I say mud?
No, that would most likely raise up some bad blood
So Sea we will call it – yes, Southend-on-Sea,
For then I feel certain we shan't disagree;
Besides it quite true is, – at least when the flood
Tide has flowed over those flats of – well – mud"
JFTW 'A Lay of Canewdon Hall', *1881*

A desolate region, it can seem, where life is bleak and harsh, and health uncertain, as Defoe commented in his description of the lives and early deaths of the farmers' wives in the Dengie Hundred in the eighteenth century. John Scott of Amwell reinforces this view of the marshland health hazard when he warns, some fifty or so years after Defoe:

"The bleak, flat, sedgy shores of Essex shun,
Where fog perpetual veils the winter sun;
Though flattering Fortune there invite thy stay,
Thy health the purchase of her smiles must pay."
John Scott 'Rural Business' *from* Eclogue 2, *1778*

But the combination of saltwater and mud, which makes up the Essex saltings, provided the environment in which many salt-loving plants grow and thrive:

"... horned poppy, sea rocket, sea kale and saltwort, together with various species of orache and sea spurge, the flora of the wide stretch of 'saltings' include golden and marsh samphires, thrift, sea lavenders, sea aster, sea brite and scurvey grass, whilst waste ground and banks near the sea are well supplied with pepperworts, sea campion, sea lettuce, asparagus, sea wormwood and wild celery, etc."
J Charles Cox Little Guides, Essex, *1909*

Here also sea birds live and feed:

MARSHLAND AND ESTUARY

"It is low tide. The long mud flats stretch out to sea. The glitter of sand sparkles as the water laps gently against the sandbanks. The chatter of wet seaweed, and the tap of an oyster catcher's bill as it hammers at an oyster shell. Swishing of air as a cormorant flutters on to a buoy. Screaming and shrieking duck fly towards the marshes. The call of Brent geese can be heard as they prepare for their long flight south."
Timothy Pyle We Live in Essex, *1978*

As the saltings grew high and solid and the vegetation became established, good pasture emerged – especially for sheep, and the dreary desolate pictures of unwholesome mud and water gave way to warm sunlight and busy life.

"Down on Tollesbury Marshes
That is where I wish to be,
Where the purslane and the grasses
Meet the high-roads of the sea;
Where the bees across the saltings
Feed on lavender and light,
And the barley ripe for malting
Climbs the camber of the dyke.

Where the butterflies are brimming
On the bounty of the hedge,
Through the golden air are swimming
Over thistle-down and sedge;
Like a carnival that clamours
Through the cavalcade of clays,
Every colour's wing a banner
On the brine-bedazzled haze."
Mervyn Linford 'Tollesbury Marshes', *1984*

And the scene is especially idyllic in June:

"Early summer or late spring?
it is a matter of names only,
this is the loveliest of seasons.
By the slow estuary, under a huge sky,
hear the perpetual hush hush of the rushes,
contemplate the aerial ballet of the tender grassheads
a foot above the eye, and mark against the sky
the eight-foot sentinel grasses.

MARSHLAND AND ESTUARY

See here in this loveliest season
the hundred shades of green
the subtleties of yellow, the rarer reds,
learn how the blue sky alters
from zenith to level distances far as Cathay.
Frederick Vanson 'June by the Estuary', *1980*

The mention of Cathay brings with it romantic associations of the East, and of trading in exotic goods. In the past these may have been brought in illegally past the careful scrutiny of the Excisemen, as S L Bensusan records:

"Com wi' rum, an' gin, an' bacca, an' lace, same's what wimmen wear in Lunnon. Lord! I weren't on th' marsh wi' me sheepses f'r nothin'. There's many things I seed, being' very 'eedful ... It's many a cargo I've seed run up the river; an' when I were a young man, 'twerent 'Cisemen nor Reveny cutters, neigher, what could stop they. The boats used to come up wi' the toide, an' drop th' stuff wi' floats and sinkers, an' then out they'd goo agen; an if chance toimes they met a Reveny cuttor, they was just 'hard workin' fisherfolk what 'adn't never done no 'arm to nobody. An' then th' little boats'd put out o'ere an' bring the'stuff ashore, an' bury some on it, an' take the rest inland wery slow like an' careful. Lord! I've knowed th' Ciseman to come a-gallopin' down th' road, an a score of' bar'ls under th'hedge right in sight, if it 'adn't bin so dark, th' fools!"
S L Bensusan A Countryside Chronicle, *1907*

But as Hilda Grieve said in *The Great Tide*, "Essex and the sea have been antagonistic", and the sea can be a pitiless and dangerous enemy to Essex folk. In his poem 'Estuary', John Abrahams tell of the drowning of a young boy off the coast, linking it in imagery with Shakespeare's play *The Tempest*:

"Several horizons; the sea wall; the sky;
And the creeks
Which betray;
Which at low tide are paddling pools:
Which at mid-tide challenge the adventurous:
Which at high tide strand and drown.
His name was Colin, he was seven or eight,
He stuck in the mud and drowned, from the water.
Sunk into the mud,
Into the worm-casts and crab-shells,
The pearl disintegrated,

IMAGINED LAND

The illuminated sea-mist of the estuary
Covered the memory of the pearl."
John Abrahams 'Estuary', *1988*

Much more graphic and matter-of-fact is the account by Robert Malster of the death of seventeen year old George Lewington, from Grays, in the wreck of the ketch, 'Days'. She was on her way up the coast from London to Sunderland in December/January 1890-91 when she struck the Cork Sand off the Essex coast:

"The worst is over (the skipper) thought. But a minute or two later there was a crash as she struck heavily on another part of the sand, and when the skipper dashed below to get a light he found himself up to the waist in water. He and his two companions tried to launch their small boat, but the waves caught it and smashed it against the billyboy's side and stove it in. As the wreckage of the little boat was carried away by the swirling waves the ketch sank beneath them. All three climbed into the port rigging, the skipper lashing the youngster near him so that he would lean over and try and warm him by rubbing his face and hands. 'George, keep up lad, the lifeboat's coming,' the skipper told him. But no lifeboat came, and after they had clung to the rigging for five long agonising hours the boy died. It was not until dawn that the light-keepers aboard the Cork lightship spotted the wreck and signalled for the lifeboats."
Robert Malster Wreck and Rescue on the Essex Coast, *1968*

A dangerous, yet rewarding, part of Essex is its coast, depicted in literature as an area with a close relationship between man and nature, where man's efforts to control and civilise, to enjoy and master, are at times thwarted by the strength and cussedness of nature:

"In front, thousands of acres of grey mud where grew dull, unwholesome looking grasses. Far, far away on this waste, two tiny, moving specks, men engaged in seeking for samphire, or some other treasure of the ooze-mud. Then the thin, white lip of the sea and beyond its sapphire edge in the half-distance the gaunt skeleton of a long-wrecked ship. To the north, on the horizon a line of trees; to the west, over the great plain, where stood one or two lonely farms, another line of trees. On the distant deep some sails and in the middle marsh, a barge gliding up a hidden creek as though she moved across the solid land. Then, spread like a golden garment over the vast expanses of earth and ocean, the flood of sunshine, and in our ears the rush of the north-west gale and the thrilling song of larks hanging high above the yellow, salt-soaked fields. Such seemed the Dengie Marsh as I saw it in June 1901. But what must it be like when buried beneath the snows of winter, or when the howling easterly winds of spring sweep across its spaces, and the combers of the North Sea sometimes reach and batter their frail embankment?"

H Rider Haggard Rural England, *1902*

The forest

WE KNOW WHERE Epping Forest is, more or less, but where is the Forest of Essex, or, for that matter Waltham Forest, Wyntreye, Writtle or Kingswood? Where Hainault, where Hatfield? All, before the mid-fourteenth century, were part of the great Forest of Essex that covered almost the whole of the county. Partial disafforestation in 1204 took the area to the north of Stanestreet, the road between Bishop's Stortford and Colchester, and by the mid-fourteenth century the Forest had been confined to the south-west corner of the county and was known as Waltham Forest. This name persisted until the second half of the seventeenth century and since then Epping Forest has dominated our thoughts and imagery.

The Forest originally had little to do with trees. Trees dominated the Essex landscape everywhere; the Forest was an area reserved for the King's hunting where no one, not even the haughtiest baron or bishop, might hunt without the king's permission, where no one might grub up land or build a hovel without a licence, or pay a fine, where the Forest law subsumed the Common Law and only the rights of commoners were protected. Now we think of the trees.

> "The legal boundary of Waltham Forest enclosed 60,000 acres, of which the present Epping Forest is 6,000. But Epping Forest is not a fragment of its former extent; it has never been much larger than it is now ... The difference is due mainly to a change in the meaning of the word, from the legal to the physical Forest. Over three-quarters of the 60,000 acres have always been ordinary Essex countryside – farms, hamlets, ordinary woods, parks and a town (Waltham Abbey) – in which the deer, should they stray, were still protected by Forest Law."

Oliver Rackham The History of the Countryside, *1987*

Instead of seeing Epping Forest as a once working area we now think of it in terms of walking and recreation in the midst of growing trees, beech, hornbeam, holly, oak and alder; cattle are too valuable to be risked by letting them loose to graze the coverts. William Morris saw the forest change:

> "When I was a boy, and for long after, except for a piece about Queen Elizabeth's Lodge, and for the part about High Beech, the Forest was almost wholly made up of pollard hornbeams mixed with holly thickets. But when the Corporation of London took it over about twenty-five years ago, the

topping and lopping, which was part of the old commoners' rights, came to an end, and the trees were let to grow."
William Morris News from Nowhere, *1891*

The forest is an interesting area with its cultural and literary associations as it brings together a complexity of memory, nostalgia and instinct:

"The past has life in the Forest. Nowhere is it easier to imagine the long pageant of history than against the unchanging scene of heath and woodland, with a herd of frightened deer leaping into cover. Time is no longer fenced into patterns and periods."
William Addison Epping Forest, *1945*

and, as Jay Appleton observes in *The Poetry of Habitat*, "The craving of modern man for trees and vegetation of all sorts is an expression of longing for what was originally natural habitat, a place which furnished food and shelter". But that place of comfort and refuge could, and still can, quickly become a place of danger, and travelling in or through the forest can present the traveller with hazards:

"Travellers through its dark and overgrown paths were wont to meet, if they met anybody, not lovers at play in a sylvan paradise, but ruffians or gangs of ruffians intent upon relieving them of money and goods. In woods as thick and extensive as those of Waltham Forest the limited number of patrolmen and keepers could not locate and entrap every rogue and vagabond."
Harold Priestley Essex Crime and Criminals, *1986*

Priestley, with typical literary creativity, goes on to mention a particularly notorious band

"known as the Waltham Blacks, from the practice of blacking their faces when on the prowl. Men like these, augmented by numbers of ex-soldiers discharged from the army after the wars in the Netherlands and elsewhere with no means of support, had their secret haunts there. At pistol-point they commandeered horses, becoming mounted irregulars, lords of the wild, terrorising or tempting innkeepers and householders near the Forest to provide shelter and storage space for their gains. Any traveller taking the Cambridge or Bishop's Stortford Road did so in peril of losing possessions, life and limb."

(*ibid.*)

THE FOREST

The Waltham Blacks actually terrorised forests in Hampshire, but the sentiment is true and, as everyone knows, Dick Turpin, born in 1706 at Hempstead near Saffron Walden, has become an Essex Forest legend for jumping five-barred gates and for his love of his faithful steed, Black Bess, as invented by Harrison Ainsworth in his novel *Rockwood*.

It is this same rich depth of history, scenery, legend, atmosphere and reflection that comes through descriptions of the forest, such as this from the 'Forest' section of Mike Shield's poem:

"It was mildest December
when I walked its wide, contrasting spaces,
ducked cantilever branches,
scuffed copper-alloy mould
from beeches pillaring the clouds:
with castellated chalice of trunks,
large old elm, larch,
arthritic oaks
and pines longing for the light.

And I was aware, too,
among these aged trees, of how
beneath the crackling cover
deep-rotting roots of ancestors
burrowed to the bedrock,
an archaeology of vegetation,
and saw how ancient primitives
heard spirits whisper here,
saw goblins in the convoluted bark,
smelt monsters in the dwarf-stump outcrops,
and feared the witchwood.

So I faced again my own preoccupation,
felt the past present itself to me,
tying me numb and dumb and wordless
in among the woods and weeds
and leaves leaving largesse for next year's growth,
knowing that I must escape that I might make
my poem, for, with silence and with savage age,
this forest swamped the song
it made me sing."

Mike Shields 'All the Slain Soldiers', *1980*

The forest then is a powerful and even sinister place for some writers; though others see it in a positive, exuberant way, focusing on the beauty and variety of the vegetation and wildlife, and, for John Clare, the birds in particular:

"I love to hear the Nightingale -
   She comes where Summer dwells -
Among the brakes and orchis flowers,
   And foxglove's freckled bells ...

The redcap is a painted bird,
   And sings about the town
The Nightingale sings all the eve
   In sober suit of brown.

I knew the sparrow could not sing;
   And heard the stranger long:
I could not think so plain a bird
   Could sing so fine a song.

I love the Poet of the Woods,
   And love to hear her sing, -
That, with the cuckoo, brings the love
   And music of the spring."
John Clare 'Nightingale at High Beach', *1841*

or, for John Davidson, the weather:

"High above the wind the clouds at rest
   Emptied every vat and steeply hurled
Reservoirs and floods; the wild nor'west
   Raked the downpour ere it reached the world;

Part in wanton sport and part in ire
   Flights of rain on ruddy foliage rang;
Woven showers like sheets of silver fire
   Streamed; and all the forest rocked and sang."
John Davidson 'November: Epping Forest', *1905*

John Clare and John Davidson may show us the forest in different seasons and in different moods, but both present a place where observation and reflection are necessary to capture the essence of the surroundings. And so the forest has become

THE FOREST

a place for contemplation, recreation and enjoyment, especially as London with its noise and bustle creeps nearer. A threat that Clare pondered upon in his poem, 'London versus Epping Forest':

"Thus London, like a shrub among the hills,
Lies hid and lower than the bushes here.
I could not bear to see the tearing plough
Root up and steal the Forest from the poor,
But leave to Freedom all she loves, untamed,
The Forest walk enjoyed and loved by all!"

Unlike the sea, the forest has a particular character within a particular area of the Essex landscape, and has almost a man-made quality that makes it manageable and amenable for the pleasure and recreation of those who appreciate

"The loveliest forest in the world – not equal to what it was, but still the loveliest forest in the world, and the pleasantest, especially in summer; for it is then thronged with grand company, and the nightingales, and cuckoos, and Romany chals and Chies (boys and girls). As for the Romany-chals there is not such a place for them in the whole world as the Forest ... It is their trysting place, as you would say, and there they muster from all parts of England, and there they whoops, dances and plays, keeping some order nevertheless because the Rye of all the Romans is in the house, seated behind the door."

George Borrow Romany Lavo-Lil Word-book of the Romany, or English Gipsy Language, *1874*

Especially since the coming of the railway, the forest has become a place to visit and enjoy – a place of natural beauty and colour, of enchanting wild life and sound:

"He booked to Epping Street ...
A purple haze that scarce could keep
Diaphanus consistence spread
Above the ridged perspective deep
Of Epping Forest; overhead
With arabesque of shining thread
As manifold as jewelled dyes,
In varied beauty interwed
A snowy vapour damaskwise
Endued the tenderest of turquoise skies.

A doe stepped forth and about
With wondering look and watchful ear,
Then vanished. Venturous birds burst out
As in the heyday of the year
With summer song in snatches, clear
As water dropping in a well;
Harmonious from a turret near
Replied a silvery vesper-bell;
The braided light grew golden; evening fell."
John Davidson from 'Railway Stations', *1908*

The forest in all its aspects can provide a richness of worlds — of nature and people, of past and present, of youth and age, of memory and nostalgia. And all these are gathered together in Edward Thomas' reflections, which are individual but also universal:

"Down each green road a cottage looks at the forest.
Round one the nettle towers; two are bathed in flowers.

An old man along the green road to the forest
Strays from one, from another a child alone.

In the thicket bordering the forest,
All day long a thrush twiddles his song.

It is old, but the trees are young in the forest,
All but one like a castle keep, in the middle deep.

That Oak saw the ages pass in the forest,
They were a host, but their memories are lost.

For the tree is dead: all things forget the forest
Excepting perhaps me …"
Edward Thomas 'The Green Roads', *1916*

Champion country

WHILE THE MARSHES have a natural boundary in the sea, and the forest had its legal boundary set for the implementation of its particular laws, the champion country has no such definite boundary and can best be defined as central and north-west Essex:

"The deepest Essex few explore
   Where steepest thatch is sunk in flowers
And out of elm and sycamore
   Rise flinty fifteenth-century towers."
John Betjeman 'Essex', *1954*

This is possibly the area of Essex that is the most closely associated with the fictional idea of a picturesque England, of an arcadian Golden Age of landscape where hills roll gently, valleys nestle quietly, streams meander musically, and trees, flowers and birds form a natural environment in harmony with man; an area presented to the world with pride:

"And when he has crossed from the east to the west,
From the north to the south – he'll agree that the best
Of the county is found in its far north-west corner;
Though to state this, of course, will rouse many a scorner.

For those who dwell eastward or south in the shire,
Will probably say that truth doth require
To give equal honours to east as to west;
But, no, I repeat it: this corner is best.

We think of its valleys, which run to and fro,
We remember its streams, and their musical flow;
Of its chalk hills and hamlets, which lie in between –
An abundance of charms which colour each scene."
Albert J Treloar 'The Chalk Hills of Essex', *1928*

It is also an area where the times and seasons, linked with man's activity, create a scene of pleasure and contemplation, in this case around Thaxted:

IMAGINED LAND

"The wheat has grown inches high
In a few days since I came by;
The meadows glow a deeper green
Where the April rain and warmth have been.

I never saw a finer sight
Than this rich earth, where flints shine white
In patterns where the plough has made
The waves of red-gold light and shade.

An evening peace enfolds the land
And in the sky's caressing hand
Wakes the first primrose Star; a Lark
Cascades his dazzling song against the dark."
Douglas Gibson 'Essex Evening', *1975*

There are panoramic views from those high places in the county that provided strategic vantage points in the past, as imagined descriptively by Jesse Berridge in his novel about the Civil War in Essex:

"The Great Ridge, more than a mile long, that lifts Essex's wastes like a bulwark to lonely outlook over the distant blue hills and the waters and saltings of the Blackwater estuary, running with scarce perceptible depressions and risings on its crest from Danbury on the south due north to Little Baddow, bears poised on the latter extremity an ancient earthwork. The ground falls away on all sides but one from the circular wall, and from thence a great tract of country is visible ... Bracken and ling, scrub oak, briar and twisted thorns, decayed willows, struggle in wild growth upon the uncultivated land, to die and rot and seek sepulture beneath the fine gravel and silvery sand and loam whereof the undulating slopes and valleys are composed. Water stays suspended in quiet little pools and marshy tracts on the higher levels, or finds it way slowly amid the 'mares' tails' in the deep valleys, and the ground is perforated by numbers of rabbits.'
Jesse Berridge The Stronghold, *1926*

These high places, no longer so strategically important, still give us those satisfying horizons that are so important to people for "Nothing in the landscape ... so powerfully evokes ... fascination and ... pleasure as the horizon" (Jay Appleton *The Symbolism of Habitat*). And these satisfying horizons are described clearly and plainly by David Smith in his account of life in West Hanningfield:

"When the last outlying cottages are past and the Galleywood road is only one hundred yards away, any one who stops and turns about may see that rare phenomenon in Essex, a real long-distance view. In front the land slopes away over the Hanningfields into blue distance, and to the right, it seems, almost to the Thames estuary and the Kent hills."
David Smith No Rain in those Clouds, *1943*

and more dramatically by John Clare:

"I love the breakneck hills, that headlong go,
And leave me high, and half the world below."
John Clare 'A Walk in the Forest', *1841*

To many, this part of Essex is seen as the centre of the agricultural and farming community. It is an area where both the 'soft' and the 'hard' view of the pastoral scene can be observed. There is the consciously literary lyrical view of Spike Mays:

"Throughout the day they would paint the golden backcloth of stubbles with long dark stripes of turned earth which got wider and wider until ploughmen were almost within reach of each other and until all the gold had been turned into rich dark brown. Birds would follow the ploughs, pecking out grubs from the newly turned earth, fighting and wheeling in the air, shrieking and singing for the joy of new-found food. Rooks and blackbirds — the greedy ones — would stay in the furrows, walking and eating behind the ploughs until so gorged they were too heavy and fat to fly."
Spike Mays Reuben's Corner, *1969*

Compare the more down-to-earth realistic comments of Isaac Mead, reflecting on the ups and downs of all life, including country life:

"The course of life is ever pleasure and trouble, day in and day out. Life is like the weather — continual changes. This is for our good. The man that never meets with a day's illness never thoroughly values health. The man that is never really hungry does not appreciate food; so if we never met with troubles we should all be lopsided, and never have any sympathy for anyone ... Country life is one continual change. We plough a field and sow some fine seed; plenty of manure is put on, everything looks lovely; prices promise to be favourable. Then just as one is about to reap the rewards of one's toil, down goes the whole thing. That which looks like being the means of enjoyment is a failure."
Isaac Mead The Life Story of an Essex Lad, *1922*

IMAGINED LAND

But not every year was a failure, and the region has been, and still is, thought of as fertile and prosperous:

"From Colchester to Ipswich and thence to Dedham the way pretty good except 4 or 5 miles they call the Severalls, a sort of deep moor ground and woody ... and now I go into Suffolk which is not so rich a land as that part of Essex I passed through which was meadows and grounds with great burdens of grass and corn."
Celia Fiennes Through England on a Side Saddle in the Time of William and Mary, *published 1888*

A region also that satisfies environmental interests in the natural world. John Ray (1627-1705) from Black Notley, one of the founders of modern botany and a great naturalist, was fascinated by the variety of plants in Essex:

"Undoubtedly the most interesting plant of Essex is the true or Bardfield oxlip (primula elatior). It is a beautiful primula and ought not to be confounded with the various hybrids between the cowslip and the primrose ... There are three flowering plants said to be found nowhere else but in special localities in Essex. They are the sickle-leaved hare's ear which are abundant in parts of the Ongar district ... the red flowering Fyfield pea, found only in cornfields at Fyfield ... and a variety of bedstraw, termed small-fruited goose grass ... which has spread over a wide district round Saffron Walden, particularly in potato fields."
J Charles Cox Little Guides, Essex, *1909*

His was a specialist interest, but Spike Mays, in the story of his Essex childhood, furnishes us with detailed observation of the multitude of life in the hedgerows around Ashdon:

"Those hedgerows were eye-openers. They were full of interest apart from the many small creatures sheltering and feeding in them. They were made up of a great variety of plants with their own characters and habits. These included great yellow tassellings of the hazel, the male flowers and, on the same shrub, those tiny flower-tips of the female – waiting for the hedger, birds, bees or beasts, to shake down the pollen from the drooping yellownesses, to fertilize them and bring forth the hazel nuts. They also included the angular twigs of the elder, the first shrub to put forth its tooth-edged leaves, the nice straight growths of new wood between the nodal joints, all full of frothy pith, just waiting for young lads to make pop-guns from them. Then there were dogwood, privet, hawthorn, black-thorn, sloe and crab-apple ..."
Spike Mays Reuben's Corner, *1969*

while other writers remind us that we often use features of the landscape to comment on our own individual thoughts and experiences, especially those connected with the passage of time and hope for the future:

> "Whispering together, summer on summer, these aspens
> Have seen much come and go
> In the eighty years or so
> Since they first lifted from the Essex soil
> Their tossing leaf-talk.
> Once they were young amid rough fields
> By a rough farmhouse, set in mud and droppings ...
> Only later came the sisters, when these aspens
> Had gossiped and sibillated for a generation of men or more,
> And the house grew, the rutted yard
> Became a drive. About them a garden
> Took shape under the spades of the brides of Christ ...
> Whispering together summer on summer the aspens
> Remember time and change in this corner of Essex quiet,
> Content as the Sisters in their lot are,
> Whispering together in service and prayer."
>
> *Frederic Vanson* 'The Aspens' *from* Hemingford Grey and other Poems, *1980*

> "Oh infinite to me
> The wonder of all this,
> The beam of light, the soil,
> Straight furrows and long toil,
> The turning beam of gold
> Sweeping the long night field
> What hope and faith it told."
>
> *Peggy Whitehouse* 'Latchingdon Fields', *1980*

Townscapes

ESSEX IS A county of villages not of towns, charming not grand. The greatest urban spread is nineteenth century (now lying in five London Boroughs in what was the south-west of the county) yet no town has ever dominated this land. West Ham was one of the fastest growing towns in the world in the second half of the nineteenth century, a wild west of a place which made Tombstone seem orderly and seemly, but it was East Ham which, with its Town Hall (1901-1903), Technical College, Public Library and Police Station (1904) best reached towards a proper town centre. Here the County administration has lost control, and from here to Loughton and to Havering, but many of us still like to think of the whole area as Essex and not London in Essex. Now Southend is the greatest conurbation, yet how many of us ever think of it as a town? A seaside watering place, possibly, a Clacton on the Thames, a place of leisure and pleasure and ice-cream and chips but can we claim it to be a place of separate character and proud individual identity? Basildon and Harlow, the county's grand 'new towns', and Chelmsford, the county town (but has that given it any distinction?) are all, in national terms, small. Even Colchester, which has retained an architectural continuity marking it out from all other centres in Essex, only just manages to cross the threshold of population which might mark a town today. It is hardly surprising that writers have tended to concentrate on the small town as a symbol of the disappearance of traditional ways of life, the vanishing of familiar beloved countryside (what is south-Essex without its elms?), the appearance of hard streets, roads and buildings, not slummy, of course, but on no soul-uplifting scale:

> "Thanks to industrial Essex
> I have spun on the greasy axis
> Of business and sociometrics;
> I have come to know the structures
> Of public service
> As well as I know the doves
> Crop-full in mildewed haycocks.
> I know that what they merit
> Is not scorn, sometimes scorn
> And hatred, but sadness really.
>
> Italic on chalky tussocks,
> The devious lovely weasel,

Snakes through a privileged annex,
An enclave of directors.
Landscapes of supertax
Record a deathful failure
As clearly as the lack
Of a grand or expansively human
Scale to the buildings of Ilford.

The scale of that deprivation
Goes down in no statistics."
Donald Davie 'Thanks to Industrial Essex.' *1969*

Colchester is Essex's one true town, a proper Roman hill-top town with vistas of countryside from the High Street spine, truly *urbs in rure*, within its almost complete Roman and medieval walls.

"This Town stands upon the North-side of a fine Eminence, rising gradually from the River Colne, which waters the North and East sides of it, to a height of about one hundred and twelve feet above the Surface of the River. By that means agreeable Prospects appear on every side, some extending even several miles into the country. And that position greatly contributes, at the same time, to the Healthfulness, as well as Pleasantness of the place."
Philip Morant The History and Antiquities ... of Colchester, ed. J S Appleby, *1970*

Yet this pleasant town has not stirred the literary imagination; there is no great literature about Colchester as place. Even Defoe describes the people alone and, except for him, little is worth quoting. Many writers have lived here, yet no one seems to have been moved to describe it.

"Colchester, about the year 1800, was for the young Taylors 'a very Elysium.' There were the Strutts, the Hills, the Stapletons: there was poetry, philosophy, engraving. For the young Taylors were brought up to work hard, and if, after a hard day's toil upon their father's pictures, they had slipped round to dine with the Strutts, they had a right to their pleasure ... One of the Strutts knew James Montgomery, and there was talk, at those gay parties, with the Moorish decorations and all the cats – for old Benn Strutt was a bit of a character: did not communicate; would not let his daughters eat meat, so no wonder they died of consumption – there was talk of printing a joint volume to be called *The Associate Minstrels*, to which James might contribute. The Stapletons were poetical, too. Moira and Bithia would wander over the old town wall at

Balkerne Hill reading poetry by moonlight. Perhaps there was too much poetry in Colchester in 1800."

Virginia Woolf The Common Reader, 1st series, *1925*

Foreigners and outsiders were keener to describe the place. Schellinks travelling in England, accompanying Jacques Thierry and his young son, and making his topographical drawings, best known through the Van der Hem Atlas, described the town when he stayed there on 18 July 1661 though even he had to concentrate on the people.

"Colchester, ... went to stay at the King's Head an excellent inn, where we were extremely well treated ... then went to look at the town, which is quite large, but not very neat, the churches, houses and the castle were badly damaged in the war between the king and parliament. Colonel Goring was then in command of the town, which, after a three month's siege, was forced by hunger to surrender, having survived by eating cats, dogs, rats and mice. Sir Charles Lucas, an ardent royalist, was executed, having been condemned by a court-martial in the very room in which we had our meal, a big place decorated in the English style. Colchester has a big trade in baize and woollen goods which are in much demand, and which is widely exported.

N.B. On coming into the town we saw in passing a very old man chained to a post in the street, with heavy iron rings round his neck and feet, his feet locked together and with a chain fixed to his neck, asking passers-by for alms to keep himself from starving, else he would die from hunger and thirst. We asked him what crime he had committed, and he answered he was only suspected of having stolen a pig."

Journal of William Schellinks' Travels in England, *1661-63*

When Celia Fiennes visited the town three decades later she found the town still in a ruined condition but with much to admire:

"... the town looks like a thriveing place by the substantiall houses, well-pitched streetes which are broad enough for two Coaches to go a breast, besides a pitch'd walke on either side by the houses, secured by stumps of wood and is convenient for 3 to walke together; their buildings are of timber of loame and lathes and much tileing, the fashion of the Country runs much in long roofes and great cantilevers and peakes; out of these great streetes runs many little streetes but not very narrow, mostly old buildings except a few houses builded by some Quakers that are brick and of the London mode; the town did extend it self to the sea but now its ruins sets it 3 mile off; the low grounds all about the town are used for the whitening their Bayes for which this town is remarkable, and also for exceeding good oysters, but its a dear place and to grattifye my curiosity to eate them on the place I paid dear; its a town full of Dessenters 2 meetings very full besides Anabaptists and Quakers, formerly the famous Mr. Stockton was minister there till he dyed."

The Illustrated Journeys of Celia Fiennes, 1685-1712, ed. C. Morris, *1972*

Whoever it was who wrote the description of Essex in 1724 (*Essex Review*, vol. vi, 1897) he too was an admirer of the clothing industry and the oysters:

"Colchester, the ancient Colonia of the Romans, and the chief town in the County. It may be three good Miles in Circumference: It hath ten Parish Churches, but none fine, tho' the Buildings in general are fair, and the Inns commodious. It is built upon the top of a Hill, with two long Streets running down to the bottom on each side, which makes me wonder how it could hold out a Siege during the Civil Wars, its Situation making it uncapable of being fortified ... This is the most populous town in the County and the most famous in England for Bays and Says; those Stuffs which we see the Nuns and Friers clothed with abroad, and of which the Spaniards carry such vast Quantities to America ... There runs a little River, with three Bridges over it, call'd Coln, by the bottom of this Town, which in three Miles Course makes their harbour called Vevnoe, where their Custom-House is kept, and their Shipping comes. Here are the best Oysters in the World, which are barrell'd and sent in great quantities to London &c. They have a peculiar Art here of candying Eringo-Roots."

While much has been written about Colchester, little can claim any literary distinction despite the hyperbole. Maldon is a beautiful little town when approached from the estuary and the red roofs seem to rush down towards the quay, all dominated by the tower and the steeple of the two main churches, but even hyperbole is missing in writings about Maldon. The favoured way to write about Maldon is prosaically and about the corruption of its politics, famous throughout the kingdom:

"I suppose Maldon was one of the most corrupt places in the county beating even Colchester, which is saying a good deal ... The day of the election. I put my awkward squad into The Blue Boar Hotel, gave them some refreshment, and instructed them on no account to go out until they had a written order from me. Up came my Tollesbury blue-jackets in a cavalcade of waggons, and at the tail of each waggon I had two men in command, so that the men should not be induced to get out at the bottom of Maldon's steep hill to be enticed into public-houses. We had an escort on each side of the stopping place, trace-horses were in waiting, and up the hill to vote went my lot of bluejackets.

IMAGINED LAND

At the Causeway, going up to Maldon, we were met by Sir Claude (de Crespigny)'s lot, a ragged lot of hungry-looking pugilists.

By noon, all my men had polled and I was standing by Poole's shop when a cart containing men came along with blue favours. The fellows were infuriated, the cart was broken up, the men rolled into the road, and a great fracas began.

Sir Claude's men seeing the row going on, came down at a sort of canter to take part in it, and you could hear nothing but the thud, thud of the exchanging blows. There was no bad blood there but the rowdiest election I ever remember proceeded to the end.

We lost by a few votes. The Heybridge Basin men came up at the last and settled it. The Liberals had bought them – we were outbid at the last."

Dr. Salter His Diary and Reminiscences, ed. Thompson, *1933*

No place in Essex is so redolent of history as Harwich, the to-ing and go-ing from which provides so much of the county's story from Dane to the present:

"The ferry-boats come and the ferry-boats go
From Harwich Old Town to Felixstowe
And from Felixstowe to Harwich Town
With its houses and streets all tumbledown.

When packed up tight in the Ferry-boat,
Do (folk) ever think of the ships afloat,
When Orwell and Stour in a merry glee
Dance on their way to the chill North Sea;
When St. Nicholas white on a thundery sky
Watches the great ships sailing by,
Do they see, where the sparkling waters meet,
The long grey ships of the Cruiser Fleet?"

Harwich Papers, ed. L. T. Weaver, *1994*

Harwich, the army's dwelling-place, and Dovercourt are inextricably combined and remind us of violent Danes, medieval fleets, Queen Isabella, the Speaking Rood, John Skelton's dream:

"Me thought I saw a ship, goodly of sail,
Come sailing forth into that haven broad,
Her tackling rich and of high apparel;
She cast an anchor, and then she lay at road."

(*ibid.*)

Queen Elizabeth I in 1561, the Armada, the Mayflower and Captain Christopher Jones, Samuel Pepys, Lord Nelson – the list of those connected to Harwich in myth and legend – is like a roll-call of English history, but we like best Harrison's description of that most Essex of trees, the elm, as a central feature of the town:

> "Of all the elms that I ever saw, those on the south side of Dovercourt in Essex, near Harwich, are the most notable, for they grow in a crooked manner, that they are almost apt for nothing but navy timber, great ordinance and beetles."
> *William Harrison* The Description of England, *1587*

Probably the best known line about any place in Essex is the other Mr Knightley's retort to Mr. Woodhouse's remark that he ought to have taken his family to Cromer for the summer holidays rather than to Southend. "If Mr Perry can tell me how to convey a wife and five children a distance of an hundred and thirty miles with no greater expense or inconvenience than a distance of forty, I should be as willing to prefer Cromer to South End as he could himself." (Jane Austen *Emma*, 1815) This reminds us that Southend is the South End of Prittlewell and also that its popularity sprang from its convenience of access and its cheapness. Most people who live within the Borough of Southend will rather speak of Prittlewell, Chalkwell or Westcliff, though in 1794 Thomas Archer recommended highly the New South-End:

> "From the broad terrace form'd upon the height,
> A most enchanting prospect yields delight.
> Here the new buildings uniformly plann'd,
> With southern aspect regularly stand ...
>
> Soon a convenient edifice shall rise
> And spacious baths and dressing rooms comprise ...
> That guests may constantly the waters use;
> And freely bathe at any hour they choose."
> *Thomas Archer* 'New South-End', *1794*

It is quite certain that Archer never thought of the 'Old Folk's Outing to Southend':

> 'Fat, farinaceous and wobbly,
> the old women took off their shoes
> and stockings to bathe their bad legs,
> white, veined and lardy

from child-bearing and years of toil.
They gathered their skirts and waded
their honest old rough-tough
horn-corned feet into the salt sea.'
Pat Croome, 1984

Would he rather have preferred this description of 'Westcliff 1953'?

"That year we bought a house close to the shore.
Bay windows, bulging from their wooden frames,
A tiny belvedere of saffron glass
That filled the hall with warm, religious light,
And roses in the garden, such a joy
When summer comes and, with the sun, the flowers.
I walked the dogs along the river shores
And watched the mist blot out the Kentish fields,
And turn the sea to sky, the sky to sea."
Kay Hayes 'Westcliff 1953', *1980*

Dorothy Gibson's 'Fishing Boats at Leigh on Sea' captures clearly the slightly melancholy feel of life on the estuary:

"Ebony boats poised midway between
apricot sea and sky,
or squat and square under fly away clouds
on a running tide;
post-impressionist boats on a smudgy dawn,
or motionless on a frozen sea
with a handful of stars:
smoke grey in ebb tide mud and mist of rain.

Little cockle boats with sturdy ribs
and solid hulks with a haul of fish
coming home through a rain of fire
from the dropping sun,
as they once came home from Dunkirk:
little fleet with a haul of courage
and of grief.

From sea and sky and boats
on a stream of coloured days

TOWNSCAPES

I have a haul of dreams,
shining and strange and sharp
as a heap of cockle shells."
Dorothy Gibson Thirty-Six Poems, *n.d.*

Clacton has not fared near so well:

"HOLIDAY AT CLACTON

Three ladies went to Clacton in the golden summer time,
A saucy little seaside place on the Great Eastern line,
And they guessed that they would surely have a holiday sublime;
   Yes they did, oh! they did, and they did. ...

With cycling trips, and other joys, the weeks soon sped along,
So I just record their parting words, and forthwith end my song -
'Goodbye! at home don't tell them quite all our goings on' -
   And they didn't, oh! they didn't, no they didn't."
Anon. Clacton-on-Sea Graphic, *18 August 1900*

The Kiss Me Quick vulgarity of the seaside is nicely captured here. Possibly we want a bit more of it in Essex to offset the growing sentiment and nostalgia for a by-gone age. A sentiment that, near to Clacton at St. Osyth, George Crabbe, two thirds of a century earlier, had expressed with wistful melancholy as he contemplated a vanishing countryside:

"And thus with gentle voice he spoke -
Come lead me, lassie, to the shade,
Where willows grow beside the brook;
For well I know the sound it made,
When dashed o'er the stony rill
It murmur'd to St. Osyth's mill

The lass replied – The trees are fled,
They've cut the brook a straighter bed:
No shade the present lords allow,
The miller only murmurs now;
The waters now his mill forsake,
And form a pond they call a lake."
George Crabbe 'St. Osyth,' *1834*

TOWNSCAPES

Yet, within about one hundred years of Crabbe, James Agate could see much of colourful beauty in Clacton and wrote about it with only a tinge of melancholy:

"Nothing that I know of can compare with the bosoms of those burnished doves which are Clacton's landladies. They live in houses coloured to match, little houses whose facades have all the chromatic delight of lemon pudding, raspberry sauce, and delicate sweets in blue and green ... The hub of Clacton is its pier. Walk to the end of this, and there, like as not, you will find the Laguna Belle, once known as the Southend Belle, and with a history of heroic service in the Dardanelles. She has just brought passengers from London – three glad hours, and it seems not an hour of that supreme and supernal joy which, Swinburne tells us, revives in remembrance the sea-bird's heart in a boy. But the great poet said nothing of the supreme and supernal melancholy if it is the return journey from Clacton you are making, and the joys left behind."

James Agate 'EGO 2', 1936

Such is the size and variety of Essex that to move from seaside to the Thames and to the Lea is to reach another land – and another people:

"The blind, wide town that saw my birth
A place of girders cranes and docks
Was all I knew of spinning earth
Except for small and scrubby parks
From whose parched grass arose no larks
But dusty chattering sparrows chirped
And squabbled by abandoned locks
Hinting at truths as yet unguessed;
A place of girders cranes and docks
Within whose small and scrubby parks
I learned to know the spinning earth
But did not hear the soaring larks
Nor sounds of creatures yet unseen
But learned how dusty sparrows chirped
Survival by abandoned locks;
And here I learned to see and hold
Small hints of beauties yet unguessed
And ways of creatures yet unseen
In that blind town that saw my birth."

Frederic Vanson 'West Ham, circa 1930'

IMAGINED LAND

Yet not two hundred years before the area was praised as a fertile rural paradise:

"Upon a fertile spot of land
Does Plaistow, thriving Plaistow stand:
The Sea, which whilom roll'd his Flood,
And hither brought the fat'ning Mud,
Has left a richness in the Soil
That well rewards the Peasant's toil ...

Potatoes now are Plaistow's Pride;
Whole markets are from hence supply'd.
Nor finer Mutton can you spend
Than what our fat'ning Marshes send.
And in our farmers' yards you find
Delicious Fowls of divers kind; ...

Around our fields bold Nimrod's Sons
With hounds, or nets or lethal guns,
Pursue the game ...

Does curious Fruit your palate please,
Profusions wantons on our trees;
The Pippin and the Windsor Pear
Grow ripe ...

Our orchards hit each taste that comes,
With Medlars, Berries, Nuts or Plums ...
How plump the Peach, nor is it small;
There Apricots, ripe to decay,
Would in your mouth dissolve away ..."

Anon. *from* 'In praise of Plaistow in the County of Essex', *1753*

To move further up the Lea and come to Waltham Holy Cross is to reach another land, one unencumbered by London's suburbs, and built to a scale which enhances what is left of the ancient abbey, celebrated by Tennyson:

"Ring out, wild bells, to the wild sky,
  The flying cloud, the frosty light:
  The year is dying in the night;
Ring out, wild bells, and let him die.

IMAGINED LAND

Ring out the old, ring in the new,
   Ring, happy bells, across the snow:
   The year is going, let him go:
Ring out the false, ring in the true.

Ring out the grief that saps the mind,
   For those that here we see no more;
   Ring out the feud of rich and poor,
Ring in redress to all mankind."
Alfred, Lord Tennyson, from 'In Memoriam', *1850*

Joseph Strutt also celebrated Waltham Abbey, but one feels that even in 1808 his language was too overblown, his nostalgia too greatly 'Norman Yoke' of the seventeenth century, emphasising the brave gallantry of the noble Harold in comparison with the dictatorial William:

"Full-orb'd, the splendid Regent of the Night,
Her journey half perform'd, serenely bright,
The fertile meadows, dank with dew, survey'd;
And winding banks in verdant pomp array'd;
Where ancient Lea invites her wanton beams,
And swells with dimpled pride the ample streams:
Her gushing floods the massy ruins lave
Of Waltham's fane, and murmur by the grave
Of royal Harold: There, his sprite beheld
The land afflicted by the oppressive geld;
Beheld indignant, when, at midnight hour,
He left the silent tomb and awful bow'r,
Encloister'd, and, with slow majestic pride,
Stalk'd o'er the pastures, and for vengeance cry'd."
Joseph Strutt 'At Waltham Abbey', *1808*

Further up the Lea and beyond into yet another land still nostalgic, but with a sense of fun, a land where chalk brings new forms to the landscape and the accident of patronage has brought Christian Socialism and people's festivals to Thaxted:

"Standing in those empty aisles, and seeing the shafts of sunlight slanting through the pillars, Holst dreamed of a festival of music that might happen there one day. He would bring his pupils, past and present, from Morley College and St. Paul's Girls' School, and they would do 'Sleepers Wake' and 'Soul, Array Thyself', and Palestrina, and Vittoria, and Purcell.

TOWNSCAPES

After the first festival of Whitsun, 1916, Holst wrote to a friend, 'It *was* a feast – an orgy. Four whole days of perpetual singing and playing, either properly arranged in the church or impromptu in various houses or still more impromptu in ploughed fields during thunderstorms, or in the train going home ..."

Imogen Holst Gustav Holst, *1938*

Still further towards Cambridgeshire, to Saffron Walden whose economic connections, as well as its church, are truly of that county. The best market town in England with its fine market place and its thirteenth century industrial area, named Saffron after the autumn crocus grown here in such amounts that in the sixteenth century the animals had only the verges and hedgerows to graze upon: Walden, the valley of the 'Welsh', for here in Saxon times there was a continuing settlement of Britons. Did the Saxons live on top of the hill where Normans were to build the church and castle, the castle built by Geoffrey de Mandeville, one of the greatest villains in the county's history? Is it only a good joke and a well-developed lie that gives us the story of the Essex Serpent?

"Near Saffron Walden, where the yellow crocus grows,
seven sober, well-respected worthies saw
(as their well-attested written statement shows)
a monstrous, short-winged serpent never seen before.
It was nine feet long, thick as a big man's thigh,
eyes sharp and piercing, teeth deadly sharp, they say,
although nobody claims they ever saw it fly,
none could match its cunning because it always got away."

Ernest Meadowcroft 'The Essex Serpent', *1977*

It says much for the wealth of Saffron Walden that the first peal of bells rung in the county was there in 1753 and that they advertised it to the world:

"To inform all Lovers and Professors of the Art of Ringing that the Society of young Ringers of this town, on Tuesday, the 25th December last, being Christmas-Day, did ring the true Peal of Grandsire Triples, composed of 148 Bobs, and two singles, which they effected in three hours and twenty minutes; and on Tuesday following, being New-Year's-Day, they compleated the same in eight minutes less than before ..."

And it says much for its modernity that it has its haiku:

IMAGINED LAND

"Grandfather traded
at the Corn Exchange- now I
read the Library."
Barbara Joy O'Brien, 1980

What of the county town – Chelmsford? The history of this town (or city?) was splendidly recorded in full detail by Miss Hilda Grieve in *The Sleepers and the Shadows* though there is little, if anything, of literary value written about it:

"The town was founded between 1199 and 1201 by a bishop of London, William of Sainte-Mere-Eglise, at Ceolmaer's ford in Essex, in the south-east corner of the bishop's rural manor of 'Chelmersford alias Bishop's Hall'. The new town, hemmed in between two converging rivers, the Chelmer and the 'Great River' or Can, was sited on the short hill running down to the bridges across them. The town and its bridges became an important stage on the highway which linked London with East Anglia and the coast, known later as the Great Essex Road. The remarkable success of a small town on a cramped site was a tribute to the acumen of its founder …

The settlers who acquired the freehold plots on offer in the new town in the early years of the thirteenth century more than realised Bishop William's expectations. Within fifty years of its creation the bishop's town, with its central position in Essex, and hospitality and services developed for travellers by its pioneering townsmen, became the county town, the place usually appointed for royal judges and officials to meet to conduct 'the king's business' in the county."
Hilda Grieve The Sleepers and the Shadows, Volume 2, *1994*

It is a special place with a great history:

"It must be a grand place that has a department store called 'Bolingbroke and Wenley', and so it is. Wandering lonely by the main gate I asked a gateman if the stands and floodlights just outside were the home of Chelmsford Town Football Club. 'Town?' he repeated, scandalised. 'Town!? We've got a cathedral! It's Chelmsford *City*.' Indeed the ground felt like a City Ground, with its grandstands each side. It could accommodate twelve thousand, but they're lucky to get twelve hundred. The last big crowd was in the late sixties, when they drew Ipswich in the FA Cup."
Tim Heald The Character of Cricket, *1986*

It is in fact cricket for which Chelmsford is most famous, even though the town spawned the second industrial revolution with its ball-bearings, electric generators and its wireless, but it was not always so:

> "For fifty years Essex played at Leyton. I love the idea of Leyton not least because it was the scene of the game's most famous batting record – the 555 that Holmes and Sutcliffe put on for the first wicket for Yorkshire against Essex in 1932. Sutcliffe made 313 and Holmes 224 not out.
>
> Just a year later they sold Leyton. The reasons given were financial though maybe they were depressed at playing on a ground where opponents scored 555 for the first wicket. For the next thirty years the county went walkabout. They continued to play occasional matches at Leyton and they also performed at Southend and Westcliff-on-Sea, at Ilford and Clacton and Chelmsford. In 1967 they decided they must have a permanent HQ and settled in Chelmsford where the club was originally founded at the Shire Hall in 1876."

(*ibid.*)

People and work

ESSEX, AS A county of small settlements and individualistic groups, is difficult to define in terms of an Essex Character or the Essex Personality. Writers, therefore, have escaped the problem by depicting or recording the activities of Essex people as separate individuals or groups associated with a special part or region of the county. Some of these Essex people have become legendary figures, such as the Fat Man of Maldon; the Earl of Oxford who, some say, wrote Shakespeare's plays; Wat Tyler, who led the Peasants' Revolt; or Will Kempe, who danced the length of the county, encountering people on the way:

"At Chelmsford, a mayde not passing fourteene years of age, dwelling with one Sudley, my kinde friend, made request to her master and dame that she might daunce the Morrice with me in a great large room. They being intreated, I was soone wonne to fit her with bels; besides, she would have the olde fashion, with napkins on her armes; and to our jumps we fell. A whole houre she held out; but then, being ready to lye down, I left her off."

William Kempe Nine Daies Wonder, *1600*

Others, though less legendary, still exhibit Essex eccentricities. The following extract, given to us by local people from the area, tells a tale of Rettendon folk:

"A poem composed by a group of men riddling potatoes on Gosses Farm, c.1927, is set out below as told by Mr Philip Judd.

THE PAGLESHAM

'Captain Daniels of "Paglesham" fame
Came to the Bridge with a load of grain
The Barge he sailed was a double-decker
Down the wall went Mr Pecker
Throw me a line said Pecker to Mears
We'll have you up and give three cheers
So up they went with a ruddy blush
Then in the "Barge" with a bloody rush
Bring me one said Pecker to Morse
Harry Mears wants one of course
Bring me one and if you're quick
I'll pay for the three said Captain Dick.

Drink it up and away we'll go
Over the road to see old Joe
See if he will unload us today
Then tomorrow we'll go away
They went away down to the chain
That was one end of the Paglesham fame
They went away that very next day
And got to London so they say
Loaded their freight with an electric crane
Then off they went to the Bridge again.'

Cast in order of appearance -
Dick Daniels – Skipper of the Paglesham
Mr. Pecker – Harry Baycock
Harry Mears – mate on the Paglesham
Morse – Mr. Fred Moss, landlord of the "Barge" (Morse was not poetic licence, but normal Rettendon pronunciation of Moss)
Old Joe – Joe Thorpe, granary foreman.
The 'chain' was a mooring chain by Little Hayes Farm."

A tale that gives little concrete information about working patterns and modes of employment, but a tale that highlights something of the puzzling liveliness and wit of the people in the area. And wit and exaggeration are combined in this account of the astounding fertility of the eight parishes of the Roothings, written about by Edward and Gunnar Johnston:

"There are many farms in the Roothings where the grain and the fruits grow to a great size. An ear of corn there is too large to be threshed with flails: each grain has to be dragged from the ear by a team of horses and then sawn into quarters in a sawmill before being ground ... In the autumn the harvesters are very busy gathering the fruit of the currant trees, but the work is very dangerous: twelve new labourers were one day standing under one of the trees, when a red currant fell on their heads and killed them."
from In Praise of Essex, ed. R. Blythe, *1988*

Often the character studies are set against a background of communal working life and a picture is then gained of a person together with a glimpse of his or her lifestyle – filtered, of course, through the imagination of the author, and so not totally reliable as a guide or manual to the type of work undertaken! Even in the classic descriptions of Virgil and Ovid there was an element of impressionist romanticism, which continues in the traditional view of the bluff, honest, hardworking countryman, from Essex or elsewhere, ready to turn out to work in all seasons:

> "But spring would follow, and summer, to compensate us in our fields. Hay had to be mown and carted ... And after the hay had been harvested, and the green of the growing grain was changing to gold, there would be knowing and appreciative looks at that welcome changing.
>
> 'Best hev a word with Toe-Rag ... Reckon we oughter fin owt how much we're likely ter git fer harvest' ...
>
> In the early weeks of August there would come an important meeting. All would gather in the cart-shed ... to 'Settle for Harvest'."

Spike Mays Reuben's Corner, *1969*

Compare the Spike Mays account of farming life in the early twentieth century with that of two other autobiographical accounts of a similar period, working in the Chelmsford and Hanningfield areas of the county. In Isaac Mead's life story, he tells of the work he put into building up a dilapidated farm, Hornets, creating the picture of a very independent, rather solitary, self-reliant man:

> "The farm, Hornets, which I last took, was in a very dilapidated state. Buildings of no value upon it, everything in a forlorn state. During the past nine years I have put in the greater part of my spare time to bring this into a more creditable condition. As I stated, I built a stable upon it, renovated a shed, and built several others, including a cattle-shed. I built a manure-shed with a loft over it, also two large cartsheds for implements. These are necessary because implements cost money, and if these stand out in all weathers they deteriorate more than they do in use. I also built a Dutch barn to hold forty acres of produce, and also a granary or corn store ... Then cleaning the land; this had all been fallow, some twice, different fields in different years. Several of the fields I was fortunate enough to get ploughed up and get the weed-seeds to germinate. One cannot kill weeds until they start to grow ... When one is fortunate enough to get these to germinate on a fallow it is an easy task to get rid of them if the weather is right. Work well done at the right time always pays, and one of the pleasures of life is to work as if each thing is the most important thing at the time that needs doing. A busy person is very often a happy person."

Isaac Mead The Life Story of an Essex Lad, *1922*

David Smith's account, on the other hand, presents not a community enterprise, nor an independent venture, but a family concern involving generations:

"The one thing the old labourers remembered about my great-grandfather, Edward Smith, was how he used to sit on the front doorstep of Link House at five o'clock in the morning during harvest time and eat his breakfast. This consisted of a quart mug of beer and a plate of cold salt pork. He seems to have worked hard and enjoyed himself. He was responsible for either chalking or liming some five hundred and sixty acres of land in West Hanningfield and used to get up along with his men at five in the morning and drive a cart himself six miles to a neighbouring village station to fetch his material. His chalked land was a great heritage for his descendants; and though this land has lain derelict for twenty year, it is now at last being brought back into cultivation, and should yield good crops."

David Smith No Rain in those Clouds, *1943*

This diversification of working backgrounds and characters is not only a feature of the agricultural areas of Essex; the sea coast and the maritime working patterns also produced a variety of work and of people:

"This Essex coast breeds a strange, fierce love of itself. It is a country for men who love solitude and the silence of the sea. Its own men, the fishermen and the fowlers, the winklers and shepherds, the bargemen and the marsh "lookers", with here and there still an ancient with gold rings in his ears and still in quiet creek-head villages, "wise women" who will charm your warts away and cure your cows, these people are a race apart. ... They are supreme individualists, fierce in independence, polite with nature's own courtesy and witty with that spontaneous wit which puts the townsman's thought-out reiterated jokes to shame ... Their names alone are guarantee of their lineage, of pedigrees longer and block more ancient than that of half the people who add strange decoration to our peerage."

J Wentworth-Day The Coast of Enchanted Wings, *1946*

Often these fierce individualists are seen against the background of the environment in which they work – the vast expanse of sea and sky:

"At low tide I watched him pad
Over the thick brown mud,
His big sea-boots
Leaving tracks
Like exclamation marks.

Further and further he walked:
I could see the spurts

IMAGINED LAND

Of water from his boots
As he went on
Towards the horizon
Where the waves shone
In the afternoon sun.

Then he was a dark blot
Moving with slow
Determination across
The vast expanse
Of mud and sea:
Strange and legendary
As in a Greek odyssey."
Douglas Gibson 'Fisherman', *1975*

And it is the hardworking individuals connected with the boatbuilding and boat maintenance industries in Essex whose work on the Harwich treadmill is recorded:

"... it brooded in silence so evil and mean,
'Til a ship of the line needing tar in each seam,
Came close on the tide and without more to do,
Attached to the crane a hauser or two.

Inside the treadmill, oft 'gainst their will,
Men had to walk and keep walking still,
To suffer the torture the ache and the pain,
Down an endless road in treadmill crane.
When its stomach was full with men in their prime,
It intoned a dirge to keep them in time.
....

'Clickety-clack goes the tongue in the hard wooden rack,
To the rhythm of feet as you take up the slack.
I'll draw this old ship from the fast flowing fleet,
If it takes all the day and skin off your feet.'
....

But at last it was over this horrible dream,
And it came in the form of an engine of steam,
That drew the ship up with such ease on the rack,
With a sweet flowing sound of the clickety-clack."
Henry G Allen 'The Treadmill Crane' *from* Harwich Humour, *n.d.*

PEOPLE AND WORK

The trials and tribulations suffered whilst working on the treadmill were those connected with work and heavy labour, but the Essex coastline also attracted visitors who came to take advantage of another Essex product – wildfowl:

"In this inlet of the sea is Osey, or Osyth Island, commonly called Oose Island, so well known by our London men of pleasure for the infinite number of wild duck, mallard, teal and widgeons, of which there are such vast flights, that they tell us the island, namely the creek, seems covered with them at certain times of the year, and they go from London on purpose for the pleasure of shooting; and, indeed, often come home very well laden with game. But it must be remembered, too, that the gentlemen who are such lovers of the sport, and go so far for it, often return with an Essex ague on their backs, which they find a heavier load than the fowls they have shot."
Daniel Defoe *Tour through the Whole Island of Great Britain, 1724-26*

Defoe's well-known account of the sad fate of the Essex women who moved from the hills to the marshland is somewhat at variance with the later picture of Essex women given in S L Bensusan's short stories, *Tales from the Saxon Shore* and *Right Forward Folks*. Several of them seem to be stalwart and redoubtable people:

"Mrs Timm, that much-married, independent and short-tempered woman looked at her fourth choice in the way that is known to marshland as 'very old-fashioned'. The weather had turned cold, Mr Timm's work calls him out early and Mrs Timm has no use of the young morning hours; their lack of comfort repels her. It is fair to note that winter treats marshland harshly. 'I'm same as a delikit woman, Bill Timm,' she said sourly, 'an' I'd have ye know it. If you wake me up every morning' same as you bin doin', you'll lay me on me bed of sickness. F'r goodness sake goo down quiet an' wash in th' scullery an' keep th' stair-door closed. Then, happen I'll git a mite o' sleep. I lay awake most half th' night and that's th' truth.' It was not the truth as Mr Timm, who does not add snoring to his vices, could have maintained on oath, but he knew better than to contradict the irate lady. Such is not the path of peace which he pursues and ensures."
S L Bensusan 'Gallivanting' *from* Tales from the Saxon Shore, *1939*

or Grammer Beagle who gets the better of the posh entrepreneur Tea Garden manageress, who has attempted to exploit Grammer and her grand-daughter:

"'I ought to explain,' she (the grand-daughter) said, 'Granny was reading about you in the Intelligencer on the day you called, when they published your portrait. You had been talking to them of the good work you were doing

round here and she guessed what you were out after. So when you made your offer Granny accepted, because my father – he is her son – said that if we gave you the place for the season we would know how to run it properly for ourselves ...You thought Granny was a simpleton ...We worked quite hard for you and you made over four hundred pounds profit in some weeks. I didn't mind because I wanted to see how these things are done. You're not out of pocket even allowing for the boards and the shed. Now Gran and I are going to see what we can do.'"
S L Bensusan 'Town v. Country' *from* Right Forward Folks, *1949*

These women were in control, unlike Old Mother Hubbard, written about by Sarah Martin of Loughton, 1768-1826, who became a slave to her dog, visiting the baker, undertaker, butcher, fishmonger, tavern, fruiterer, tailor, hatter, barber, cobbler, seamstress and hosier for all his needs and, at the end, showing her subservience to him:

"The dame made a curtsey,
   The dog made a bow;
The dame said, Your servant,
   The dog said, Bow-wow."

Poems connected with Billericay, Wickford, and St Osyth support Old Mother Hubbard's view of the multiplicity of work in the county – in the High Street:

"If you can spare a little time
I'll try and take you back,
And explain a bit what our High Street was like
Over sixty years back.

The house at the top of the street just then
Was of red brick and built quite well,
With an iron gate at the corner
Where the Infants' school mistress did dwell ...

Next we come to a Pork Butcher's shop
That was kept by a Mrs Thompson,
She sold pork pies, dripping and brawn,
And she always had on a clean apron."
Jessie A Thomas 'Billericay about 1910', *1977*

or around the town:

PEOPLE AND WORK

"Here's Carter the builder who shaves at the deal
And Wooliams the wheeler who turns at the wheel
Here's Richens the builder who sharps at the steel
And sharps people up when they're down at the heel.

There's Souda the baker who kneads at the dough
And cracks his old comrades, he does it also,
There's Smith at the foundry both courageous and bold
And old Harry Nichols who works at the mould.

Here's Dandy the frosty who stabs at the leather
And Gigney his master who talks of the weather
There's Upson the Beadle, the parson does prate
He's not very big, but lives by the great."
Trad. 'Wickford', 19th century

or in the church:

"The clergy of St Osyth
   Her rural deanerie,
No thoughtful man accuseth
   Of shameful accidie.

Each person true detects him,
   Hard worker, free from pelf;
All Brightlingsea respects him,
   The Rural Dean himself.

Great Bentley's sturdy vicar
   Will cox the boat, or row,
He never stops to bicker
   But makes his parish go."
Charles Collwyn Prichard 'The Clergy of St. Osyth', n.d.

These poems remind us that there is an enormous variety of occupations in Essex other than those connected with the farming scene, the sea coast, or gentlemanly pursuits. There is the textile industry, which is a vital part of Essex history; to educationalists an understanding of it was crucial for a full awareness of the county's life. This extract from a poetic account, written by the headmistress of the County High School for Girls in Chelmsford, describes a visit to the Courtauld Silk Factory:

"THE WEAVING SHED

As each whirling spool untwines,
Like gossamer the silken lines
Swing athwart the dazzled air,
Build fantastic structures there;
Passing, crossing, all converge,
Driven by the pulsing urge
Till the threads that gleam and glow
Are caught and laid in level low,
And the shining woof grows there
Delicate and firm and fair.
Then the human touch sets free
The mighty pent-up energy;
The looms in ecstasy controlled,
Lift and shudder, leap and hold.
The darting shuttle in its flight
Bears its line of silken light,
In and out, by let or leave,
Till its radiant flittings weave,
Swift, unerring, every line
Of the intricate gay design."

Edith M Bancroft 'The Silk Factory' *from* Land of Memory, *1953*

A laudable account of honourable and worthy work; but not all Essex folk were upright and respectable. Sir William Addison in *Essex Heyday* (1949) tells of a persistent young villain in Billericay, whose master in the end can no longer cope with him:

"Stephen had shown himself, "though young in years, of a most wicked and thievish disposition". He had done many robberies and had broken more than twenty walls. Three times he had been sent to the house of correction in Chelmsford and once to the jail at Colchester. 'But wickedness,' said the suffering Mr Noone, 'is so rooted in him there is no hope of amendment, for that he groweth from evil to worse ...' Mr Noone then begged to be 'quite released of the said boy,' adding devoutly: 'And as God, no doubt, will be pleased with so charitable an act, so shall I and mine be bound, according to duty, continually to pray to Almighty God to bless your Honours and Worships with all earthly content and heavenly happiness'."

It tends to be the lack of 'earthly content' and a neglect of 'heavenly happiness' in

everyday life that leads to a life of crime – or so Harold Priestley suggests. He cites an example of ill-gotten gains, dating from 1825 at Ingatestone Fair:

"John Horsnell of Stone End Farm, Roxwell, a married farmer with nine children, needing money to pay his rents, brought his Suffolk colt in the hope of making a sale. Sure enough a customer came along offering to pay the full asking price of £29, which he took from a large roll of banknotes, assuring Horsnell that they were sound country money payable in London.

The farmer went home well pleased.

Not until next day when a friend examined his notes did he realise how he had been fooled. The notes were on two banks and dated 1808 – 17 years old and certainly false, for they were in towns where no bank had existed or where one had failed."
Harold Priestley Essex Crime and Criminals, *1986*

Fraud, deception, confidence trickery, theft were all crimes involving a quick wit and a ready tongue, and quite often a lively and engaging personality – such as that of Owd Bill:

"He never goo to Charch, a Sunday, Bill,
Excep' he keep a larkin' all the time,
A reglar bad un, tha's what he is; still
You carn't help likin' of him all the saime.

Why, up at Mis'ley – that there poachin' fray,
I'll lay yer tuppence Bill was in the spree,
But he can olluz faike the thing some way
Afore the Magistrates, so he git free.

He done it, right enough. You woon believe
The times an' times I sin him arter hares.
I could a towd 'em thay was up his sleeve –
Nao, not the rabbits, sir, nao, nao, the snares.

Oo, he's the artfullest you ever knaowed;
He never taike no hart, not anywhere.
There's nao mistake, Bill, he's owd as owd,
He's best the very Owd-un, I declare.

PEOPLE AND WORK

Nowhere there ent a bad un t'ekal he –
I knaow there ent a bigger liar livin'
Yet when the day of Judgmen' come you'll see,
He'll faike it somewho so he git to Hiven."

Charles Edwin Benham 'Essex Ballads', *1895*

But Essex folk, on the whole, are not criminal and are, rather, noted for being independent, individual, industrious and full of life, vitality and honesty. Jonas Asplin, who was doctor at Prittlewell 1826-28 was one such:

"1827

April 19. I rode smartly to make my visit first to Shoebury, but my horse not liking to leave the Prittlewell road at the Three Ash turning I pressed him and had nearly cleared the turning, when be became so suddenly and unexpectedly restive, I was completely off my guard and thrown out of the stirrups on to the pummell of the saddle with so much violence as to render me quite shiftless and, the horse continuing to plunge and kick with the utmost force, I was thrown upon my back upon the hard gravel and received so much injury that though I was able to get up upon my legs, I had no power to move and was almost immediately obliged to lie down again which, with the assistance of a man and a boy who were hoeing in Mr Lodwick's Hall field and came to my assistance, I was enabled to do on some grass between the two roads ...

April 23. After plentiful bleeding and leeching, I am this day enabled to turn myself in bed, but still have no power to move the right leg or thigh. My bruises are most severe. Saw some patients at my bedside ..."

Arthur Brown Essex People 1750-1900, *1972*

A conscientious doctor, indeed, to make his own sickbed his surgery! Another such high-principled and dedicated personality was Elizabeth Fry, grand-daughter of Elizabeth Fry the prison reformer. She lived in Warley Lodge in the 1840s and, at the age of 15, maintained a cheerful countenance and outlook on life, despite the changes and upsets within the English Church at that time:

"1842

October 30th. Sunday. Went to Church as usual. Our sermon in the morning was on a subject, caused by the Visitation last Friday, that of reviving in the Church many old customs, which have lately fallen into disuse. Many of these decidedly border on Popery, and at a time like this, when the English Church is so much torn and agitated by contending parties and by various opinions, it is perhaps unwise to introduce these new regulations, which place too much

dependence on outward forms, not sufficiently savouring of spiritual things ... for, after all, if but in heart and deed we truly and sincerely serve and worship our Great Creator, it little matters where or how our adoration and supplication is offered or with what outward signs it is accompanied."
(*ibid.*)

Here is a reminder of the Puritan conscience and religious convictions of Essex people through the ages; traits that are linked also, whether at work or leisure, with the county's independence of thought and action, and its awareness of its roots in history. H G Wells' comment in *Mr Britling Sees It Through* that "lots of this country here has five or six hundred year old families still flourishing" is reflected in a similar way by Norman Lewis, who, despite thinking the county ugly at this first meeting, became attached to it and its people. One of these, mentioned in his article 'Essex', is Dorothea Cloate, "a member of one of the Cloate family ... About half the village used to be Cloates, but there's only five families left now."

All these aspects come together in the Essex people's love of and for their county, possibly best summed up in a sentence written by the Essex-born writer, William Morris, of another key personality in Essex history, John Ball; a comment that unites the land and the sky, the earth and the heaven that is Essex:

"I come not from Heaven, but from Essex."
William Morris A Dream of John Ball, *1888*

IMAGINED LAND

Acknowledgements

The authors gratefully acknowledge the following for their help and most generous permission to reproduce copyright material, and apologise for any errors or omissions.

Alastair Press Ltd for extracts from *In Praise of Essex,* edited by Ronald Blythe, for lines from John Abrahams' 'Estuary'; Alastair Press Ltd and the executors for extracts from James Agate's 'EGO 2' and Imogen Holst's *Gustav Holst;* Henry G Allen for extract from his own publication *Harwich Humour;* Bloodaxe Books Ltd for lines from Denise Levertov's 'A Map of the Western Part of the County of Essex'; Brentham Press for extracts from *Poet's England – 6: Essex,* compiled by John Adland, for lines from Pat Croome's 'Old Folks' Outing to Southend', Ernest Meadowcroft's 'The Essex Serpent', Charles Collwyn Prichard's 'The Clergy of St Osyth', Jessie A Thomas' 'Billericay about 1910'; Brentham Press and Routledge for Donald Davie's 'Thanks to Industrial Essex'; J H Clarke & Co (Chelmsford) Ltd. for extract from George Walker's *The History of a Little Town;* J M Dent for extracts from William Addison's *Essex Heyday* and *Epping Forest* and for extracts from David Smith's *No Rain in those Clouds;* Egon Publishers Ltd for extracts from *In Praise of Essex* edited by Frederic Vanson, for lines from Kay Hayes' 'Westcliff 1953', Barbara Joy O'Brien's Haiku on Saffron Walden, Mike Shields' 'All the Slain Soldiers', Frederic Vanson's 'West Ham circa 1930', 'June by the Estuary', 'The Aspens', Peggy Whitehouse's 'Latchingdon Fields'; Essex County Council for untitled extracts by Stephen Farrar and Timothy Pyle from *We Live in Essex;* the Essex Record Office for extracts from Arthur Brown's *Essex People 1750-1900,* Hilda Grieve's *The Great Tide* and *The Sleepers and the Shadows* and for Edith M Bancroft's 'The Silk Factory' and A G Harknett's 'Elms'; Dorothy Gibson for her poem 'Fishing Boats at Leigh-on-Sea' and her husband, Douglas Gibson's two poems 'Essex Evening' and 'Fisherman'; Granta Publications Ltd for extracts from Norman Lewis' 'Essex'; Harrap Ltd. for extract from Hervey Benham's *The Last Stronghold of Sail;* Ian Henry Publications Ltd. for extracts from Harold Priestley's *Essex Crime and Criminals;* Lavenham Press Ltd. for extract from Robert Malster's *Wreck and Rescue on the Essex Coast;* Leopard's Head Press for extract from William Addison's 'The making of the Essex Landscape' in *An Essex Tribute,* edited by Kenneth Neale; Mervyn Linford for extracts from his two poems 'Glaucous Gold' and 'Tollesbury Marshes'; Macmillan Publishers Ltd for extracts from Spike Mays' *Reuben's Corner;* Martin Secker and Warburg Ltd. for extracts from Angus Wilson's *Late Call;* John Murray (Publishers) Ltd. for extract from John Betjeman's 'Essex'; Pavilion for extracts from Tim Heald's 'The Character of Cricket'; Routledge for extracts from S L Bensusan's *Tales from the Saxon Shore* and *Right Forward Folks;* Roland and Patricia Smith for the script of the poem about 'The Paglesham'; and W T Weaver for extracts from *Harwich Papers.*

IMAGINED LAND
Index of Authors

The following are quoted or referred to in the text:

ABRAHAMS, JOHN
'Estuary'

ADDISON, WILLIAM (1905-1992)
Essex Heyday, Epping Forest, 'The Making of the Essex Landscape'
A northerner who contributed richly to the knowledge and history of Essex through his many publications and his participation in the historical and cultural life of the county.

AGATE, JAMES (1877-1947)
'EGO 2'
English critic and essayist, who wrote dramatic, film and literary criticisms for such newspapers as the Manchester Guardian and the Sunday Times, as well as essays, novels and his nine-part autobiography/diary, EGO.

ALLEN, HENRY G
'The Treadmill Crane'
Local author whose *Harwich Humour* came out in 1991.

APPLETON, JAY
The Symbolism of Habitat, The Poetry of Habitat
A writer and Professor of Geography who interprets buildings, landscape and nature in terms of aesthetic elements and values.

ARCHER, THOMAS
'The New South-End'
Author of a poetical description of New Southend and its vicinity; and a biography of Queen Victoria, published 1888.

ARNOLD, MATTHEW (1822-1888)
Extract from a letter written on a visit to Copford
Poet, essayist and inspector of schools; author of *Culture and Anarchy*, a critical account of English social and political life; and poems such as 'Dover Beach', 'Sohrab and Rustum' and 'The Scholar-Gipsy'.

ASPLIN, JONAS (1775-1842)
Extract from his diaries of 1826-28
A doctor who was brought up at Little Wakering Hall, practised in Paris for many years before resuming his practice in the Southend district, mainly Prittlewell and Rayleigh.

AUSTEN, JANE (1775-1817)
Emma
Author of six published novels and three unfinished works; lived mainly in the south and west of England.

BANCROFT, EDITH M
'The Silk Factory'
Headmistress of Chelmsford County High School for Girls

BARING-GOULD, SABINE (1834-1924)
Mehalah: A Story of the Salt Marshes
Writer and divine; rector of East Mersea 1871-81; wrote the words of the hymn 'Onward, Christian Soldiers'.

BENHAM, CHARLES EDWIN (1860-1929)
Essex Ballads
Journalist, author and artist from Colchester, whose works include books on the Essex dialect and Colchester Castle.

BENHAM, HERVEY (1910-1987)
The Last Stronghold of Sail
Writer, journalist and editor in chief of Essex County Newspapers for many years; author of several books about the lore and traditions of the East Coast, including *The Big Barges, Essex Gold, Once Upon a Tide, Essex at War.*

BENSUSAN, SAMUEL L (1872-1958)
A Countryside Chronicle, Tales from the Saxon Shore, Right Forward Folk
Journalist, music critic, author, broadcaster, his especial interest was the countryside and the rural scene. He was a member of the literary colony that flourished in the west of the county in the early 20th century.

BERRIDGE, JESSE (1874-1966)
The Stronghold
Writer of several novels, all set in Essex (*The Tudor Rose, Bettina, Brother John*) and of works on Essex puritan divines of the 17th century, Thomas Hooker, John Eliot, and on Little Baddow in the medieval period.

BETJEMAN, JOHN (1906-1984)
'Essex'
A poet whose interest in Victorian architecture, especially churches, took him around the country, and whose perceptive eye and wit caught the contemporary scene. He was Poet Laureate from 1972. His autobiography, *Summoned by Bells*, was written in verse.

BORROW, GEORGE (1803-81)
Romany Lavo-Lil Wordbook of the Romany, or English Gipsy Language
A writer, who moved to literature from the legal world, and travelled widely studying the languages of the countries he visited, and for a while acted as agent for the British and Foreign Bible Society. His works include *The Bible in Spain, Wild Wales, Lavengro, The Romany Rye* – the last two have a strong autobiographical element.

BROWN, ARTHUR (1915-)
Essex People 1750-1900
Teacher, writer and historian, with an especial interest in the working people of Essex in the eighteenth to twentieth centuries.

BURMESTER, FRANCES C
John Lott's Alice
Daughter of the Rector of Little Oakley, 1830-1875, Rev. George Burmester

INDEX OF AUTHORS

CLARE, JOHN (1793-1864)
'Nightingale at High Beach', 'London v. Epping Forest', 'A Walk in the Forest'
Son of a Northamptonshire labourer, he was a poet who lived for several years in Essex. He was a great success in London literary circles for a time, but died in obscurity back in the Midlands

COWPER, FRANK (1849-1930)
Sailing Tours

COX, CHARLES J
Little Guides, Essex
Author of various articles about Chelmsford and the county; antiquarian and historian.

CRABBE, GEORGE (1784-1832)
'St Osyth'
Born and brought up in Aldeburgh, Suffolk, he lived for a time in London before starting his career as a poet. He is best known for his long poem 'The Borough' and his poem 'Peter Grimes' that was set to music by Benjamin Britten. Sir Walter Scott called him the 'English Juvenal'.

CROOME, PAT
'Old Folks' Outing to Southend'

DAVIDSON, JOHN (1857-1909)
'November: Epping Forest', 'Railway Stations'
Poet and writer, who came from Scotland where he had been a school master, 1872-89. His later work 'Testaments' expounded a rebellious philosophy of materialism.

DAVIE, DONALD (1922-1995)
'Thanks to Industrial Essex'
University lecturer, poet and critic, he was writer in residence at the University of Essex.

DEFOE, DANIEL (1660?-1731)
Tour through the Whole Island of Great Britain
Born in Tilbury, he had a varied career as hosiery merchant, participant in Monmouth's rebellion, novelist, poet, journalist and pamphleteer. His best known works, *Robinson Crusoe, Moll Flanders, A Journal of the Plague Year* and the '*Tour*' show his liberal, humane and perceptive insight into his life and times.

DICKENS, CHARLES (1812-1870)
Great Expectations
Son of a government clerk, he had an uncertain childhood and became one of the most famous novelists of the 19th century. Many of his works are set in London and area, including Essex. They include *Oliver Twist, A Christmas Carol, A Tale of Two Cities, Barnaby Rudge, Little Dorrit*.

DRAYTON, MICHAEL (1563-1631)
'Polyolbion'
Born in Warwickshire, he was a prolific poet in his time, producing collections such as 'Poems Lyrick and Pastoral'.

FARRAR, STEPHEN
Untitled poem from collection 'We Live in Essex'

FIENNES, CELIA (1662-1741)
Extract from 'Through England on a Side Saddle in the Time of William and Mary' Granddaughter of the first Viscount Saye and Sele, most details of her life come from her Journal, first published in an incomplete version in 1888, which gives an enthusiastic and lively glimpse of England during the reigns of James II, William and Mary, and Anne.

FRY, ELIZABETH (1827-1856)
Extract from diary of 1842
Grand-daughter of Elizabeth Fry, the prison reformer, she lived as a child and young person at Warley Lodge.

GIBSON, DOROTHY (1915-)
'Fishing Boats at Leigh on Sea'
A poet who has lived in and written about Essex for many years. She sees the delight and melancholy of the county's land and seascapes. Her work, like her husband's, has been published in various periodicals, magazines and newspapers.

GIBSON, DOUGLAS (1910-1987)
'Essex Evening', 'Fisherman'
A poet who wrote of the times and seasons of Essex with sensitive insight and telling detail, and who lived in the county for many years.

GRIEVE, HILDA (1913-1993)
The Great Tide, The Sleepers and the Shadows
Historian and writer, whose work as archivist at the Essex Record Office enabled her to record and write about aspects of the county with verve, vitality and lively detail.

HAGGARD, H RIDER (1856-1925)
'Rural England'
Author of adventure romances, such as *King Solomon's Mines*, he was also an acute observer of the social scene in England at the turn of the century, especially of the poor conditions of the agricultural labourer.

HARKNETT, A G
'Elms'

HARRISON, WILLIAM (1534-1593)
Description of England
Writer and topographer, who was Rector of Radwinter 1559-93, and Canon of Windsor.

HAYES, KAY
'Westcliff 1953'

HEALD, TIM
The Character of Cricket
A journalist with an interest in cricket, his book describes various county grounds with wit, humour and enthusiasm.

HOLST, IMOGEN (1907-1984)
Gustav Holst
Daughter of Gustav Holst, she was a musical educationist, conductor and composer of folksong arrangements, closely connected with the Aldeburgh Festival, and a frequent visitor to Essex.

INDEX OF AUTHORS

JUDD, PHILIP
Narrator of poem about 'The Paglesham'

JOHNSTON, EDWARD AND GUNNAR
Authors of humorous parody about Essex's fecundity.

JFTW
'A Legend of Paglesham', 'A Lay of Canewdon Hall'
A humorous writer and journalist in the county who published a collection of his writings *Essex Lays and Legends* in 1888.

KEMPE, WILLIAM (d.1603)
'Nine Daies Wonder'
Actor and comedian, who in 1599 danced from London to Norwich.

LEE, HERMIONE (1948-)
Willa Cather: A Life Saved Up
University professor, critic, broadcaster, reviewer, she has written about a number of authors including Virginia Woolf, Stevie Smith, Philip Roth and Willa Cather.

LEVERTOV, DENISE (1923-)
'A Map of the Western Part of the County of Essex'
American poet, born in Ilford of a Welsh mother and Russian Jewish father and emigrated to the USA in 1948. Her poetry, published in collections such as *Relearning the Alphabet* and *Footprints*, is radical and outspoken.

LEWIS, NORMAN (1918-)
'Essex'
Author, journalist and travel writer who captures a sense of the humanity and living environment of the places he lives in or visits, which include Essex, Latin America, Indo-China.

LINFORD, MERVYN (1946-)
'Glaucous Gold', 'Tollesbury Marshes'
A poet who has written many poems about Essex in such collections as *Two Essex Poets* (with Frederic Vanson), in which he captures, as in a picture, the evocative atmospheres and moods of different parts of the county.

MALSTER, ROBERT (1932-)
Wreck and Rescue on the Essex Coast
A writer of East Anglia whose works include histories of Felixtowe, Ipswich, Lowestoft and on various types of sailing craft. He is a member of the Society for Nautical Research.

MARTIN, SARAH (1768-1826)
'Old Mother Hubbard'
She lived and wrote in and around Loughton.

MAYS, SPIKE (1907-)
Reuben's Corner
A writer who spent his childhood in Ashdon, Essex, before moving on to Egypt and India in the Forces, then on to university and a career as a writer. *Reuben's Corner* won the Yorkshire Post Best First Work Award in 1969. His other works include *Fall out the Officers!*, *Last Post* and *The Band Rats*.

MEAD, ISAAC (1859-1923)
The Life Story of an Essex Lad
A local farmer in High Easter who wrote his autobiography about life and agriculture in the late 19th/early 20th century.

MEADOWCROFT, ERNEST
'The Essex Serpent'
A local writer of poems, plays and novels such as *In the Mood, New Poems, Stephen and Matilda*, (a historical play) and *Their name was man*, published in the 1960s and 70s.

MORANT, PHILIP (1700-1770)
The History of Essex, The History and Antiquities of the most ancient town and borough of Colchester
Writer and historian of Essex, who was curate of Great Waltham, Broomfield and Chignall and who wrote about the county, especially Colchester.

MORRIS, WILLIAM (1834-1896)
News from Nowhere, 'A Dream of John Ball'
Author, poet and craftsman who was born at Walthamstow. As a craftsman he designed and produced furniture, textiles, wallpaper, tapestries and set up the Kelmscott Press; as a writer he wrote a variety of literary works including romances and socialist texts.

NEW BRITISH TRAVELLER
General description of areas of the county.

NORDEN, JOHN (1548-1625)
Description of Essex
Writer and historian of Essex.

O'BRIEN, BARBARA JOY
Haiku on Saffron Walden
Local Thaxted poet whose work appears in *Essex Countryside* and other periodicals.

PRICHARD, CHARLES COLLWYN
'The Clergy of St Osyth'
Writer of *Daisies and Nasturtiums: Verses to boys at school and others* published c.1915.

PRIESTLEY, HAROLD (1901-)
Essex Crime and Criminals
A northerner who became a writer and university teacher, with a particular interest in Essex local history.

PYLE, TIMOTHY
Untitled poem from 'We Live in Essex'.

RACKHAM, OLIVER
The History of the Countryside
Fellow of Corpus Christi College, Cambridge, writer and researcher about the countryside, who uses much Essex material and whose works include *Trees and Woodland in the British Landscape, The Last Forest: the story of Hatfield Forest, Ancient Woodland of England: the woods of south East Essex. The History of the Countryside* won the Angel Literary Award in 1986.

SALTER, Dr
His Diary and Reminiscences

INDEX OF AUTHORS

SCHELLINKS, WILLEM (1623-1678)
The Journal of William Schellinks' Travels in England, 1661-63, published by the Royal Historical Society, 1993
Born in Amsterdam, he lived and worked there as painter, draughtsman, etcher and poet as a contemporary of Rembrandt, Hals, Vermeer and Steen. His travels through Europe in the 1660s were made as companion of Jacques Thierry, merchant shipowner, and Thierry's son, Jacques Junior.

SCOTT, JOHN
'Rural Business'

SHIELDS, MIKE
'All the Slain Soldiers'

SIZER, KATE THOMPSON
The Wooing of Osyth: the Story of the Eastern Counties in Saxon Times
Writer of historical fiction, often set in Essex and East Anglia and published in the 1880s and 90s, she lived for many years in Clacton.

SKELTON, JOHN (1460?-1529)
Poet of such works as 'Philip Sparrow', 'Why Come You Not to Court?' and 'The Tunning of Eleanor Rummyng'.

SMITH, DAVID (1913-1957)
No Rain in those Clouds
A farmer from a farming family based in West Hanningfield, he wrote about farming life and events in the first half of the 20th century, including *The same sky all over* and *Uncle Fred*.

STRUTT, JOSEPH (1749-1802)
'At Waltham Abbey'

TENNYSON, LORD ALFRED (1809-1892)
'In Memoriam'
Poet and writer who lived at High Beech 1837-40; his works included 'In Memoriam' (part of which was written while he was at High Beech), 'Poems chiefly Lyrical', 'The Lady of Shalott', 'Maud', and 'Idylls of the King'. He was Poet Laureate from 1850.

THOMAS, EDWARD (1878-1917)
'To Merfyn', 'The Green Roads'
English poet and nature writer, who was encouraged to write poetry by Robert Frost in 1914. Most of his poetry was, therefore, written during the First World War in which he was killed while on active service in France.

THOMAS, JESSIE A
'Billericay about 1910'
A local writer who published in 1973 and 1974 volumes of poetry about Billericay and its High Street.

THOMAS, KEITH (1933-)
Man and the Natural World
Formerly Professor of History at St John's College, Oxford, now President of Corpus Christi College, he has written several works on the social and intellectual background of the early modern period, including *Religion and the Decline of Magic*.

TRELOAR, ALBERT J
'The Chalk Hills of Essex'

VANSON, FREDERIC (1919-1993)
'West Ham circa 1930', 'June by the Estuary', 'The Aspens'
Local lecturer, writer and poet whose work has appeared in various journals such as *Essex Countryside*; he published more than twenty collections of verse, including *Poems Chiefly Essex, Our Lady's Tumbler, A War Age and Other Poems*.

VAUGHAN, JOHN
Lighter Studies of a Country Rector
He was born in Finchingfield; became Canon of Winchester. His work was published in 1909.

WALKER, GEORGE
The History of a Little Town
Congregational Minister in Billericay 1941-1950, he wrote and researched details of the town and area, producing the book three years before he retired to Shenfield.

WEAVER, L T (1906-)
Editor of 'Harwich Papers', and author of several works about Harwich, including *The Harwich Story* and *The Harwich Packet,* he taught at Harwich School and has held civic office in the town, including that of Mayor in 1973..

WELLS, H G (1866-1946)
Mr Britling Sees It Through
Draper, teacher and then writer, he lived in Little Easton for a number of years, an area of Essex about which he wrote in the novel. His other works include *Mr Kipps, The History of Mr Polly, The Time Machine, The War of the Worlds* and *The Shape of Things to Come*.

WENTWORTH-DAY, J (1899-1983)
The Coast of Enchanted Wings
Author, journalist and publicist who published many works about East Anglia, including *Essex Ghosts, the haunted towns and villages of Essex*.

WHITEHOUSE, PEGGY
'Latchingdon Fields'

WILSON, ANGUS (1913-91)
Late Call
A writer, member of the British Museum Library staff and Professor of English Literature, he lived for several years in East Anglia. His works include *Anglo-Saxon Attitudes, No Laughing Matter* and *As If By Magic*, in which he points up the eccentricities and foibles of the English character and behaviour.

WOOLF, VIRGINIA (1882-1941)
'The Common Reader'
Novelist, critic, essayist, publisher, her life and work was centrally linked with the Bloomsbury Group. She wrote about the art of writing, especially as perceived by a feminine author. Her books include *The Waves, Mrs Dalloway, To the Lighthouse, A Room of One's Own*.

YOUNGMAN, P
'Excursions in the County of Essex'